THE EXPERTS PRAISE *FOLLOWING THROUGH*

"A milestone among self-help books . . . indispensable reading for those cultivating positive, lasting changes in their lives."
—Ray Mulry, PhD, Author, *In the Zone: Making Winning Moments Your Way of Life*

"Finally, a book about improving performance that doesn't sugarcoat the truth. It not only calls a spade a spade; it shows you how to actually use the spade to dig in and get the job done."
—James J. Nemec, Vice-President for Agency Development, Northwestern Mutual Life Insurance Company

"Truly a pioneering work . . . filled with fascinating insights and ingenious solutions to a problem that frustrates us all."
—Ron Young, MD, Psychiatrist

"Provides the critical missing link between setting a personal goal and actually achieving it."
—Mark Larson, President, Digi-Key Corporation

"Provocative . . . ought to be read and considered by anyone serious about continuing self-improvement."
—Dan S. Kennedy, President, The Psycho-Cybernetics Foundation, Inc.

"The quintessential book about how to get it done."
—Brian Early, Executive Director of Development, Northwestern Mutual Life Insurance Company, Chicago, IL

"Eye-opening . . . takes you on a creative and compelling journey and leaves you with a new understanding of how to achieve success."
—John W. Cruikshank III, CLU, 1996–97 President, Million Dollar Round Table

"A 'must read' for anyone who's fighting the good fight to lose weight, quit smoking, or improve performance in any way."
—C. Wayne Mitchell, President, Productive Presentations, Inc.

"It's the one book that's been missing from the self-help bookshelf. And it may be the last self-help book you'll ever need."
—Peter Vandermark, Associate Professor of Journalism, Boston University

"Provides the tools you need to truly become the captain of your own ship."
—Ben Benjamin, PhD, Author, *Listen to Your Pain*

"*Following Through* will empower you to do more with your life than you ever thought possible."
—Joan Brock, Author, *More than Meets the Eye*

"If you have a dream in your heart and this book in your hand, start reading. Each page of this book will take you one step closer to having your dream come true. I guarantee it."
—Ron Gilbert, PhD, Editor, *Bits & Pieces Magazine*

"As a consultant to global leaders in high-tech, health-care, and financial services, I see the problem of poor follow through rob my clients of success every day. Fresh, clear, and powerful, this book is jam-packed with exciting new solutions to an age-old problem."
—Gil Williams, Partner, Rheault-Williams Consulting

"Required reading for my entire sales force! Full of original concepts and practical techniques for taking control of your personal destiny."
—Harry P. Hoopis, President, Hoopis Financial Services

"Creative and practical solutions for important everyday problems . . . revealed with wit, wisdom, and warmth."
—John Tyler, PhD, CEO, Human Resources Consultants

FOLLOWING THROUGH

STEVE LEVINSON, Ph.D.
& PETE GREIDER, M.Ed.

Kensington Books
http://www.kensingtonbooks.com

KENSINGTON BOOKS are published by

Kensington Publishing Corp.
850 Third Avenue
New York, NY 10022

ISBN 1-57566-348-1

First Printing: October, 1998
10 9 8 7 6 5 4 3 2

Printed in the United States of America

To all the good intentions
that needlessly died so young

ACKNOWLEDGMENTS

Lots of people helped us follow through with *Following Through*.

First, we'd like to thank our literary agent, Barbara Bova, and our editor at Kensington Publishing, Tracy Bernstein, for sharing our vision of a book that aims to change forever the way people think about and treat their own good intentions. Barbara and Tracy applauded rather than flinched when we proposed to make hamburger out of some of the self-improvement industry's most sacred cows.

Thanks to John Gunstad, psychologist-to-be and volunteer extraordinaire, for the many careful interviews and insightful observations. Thanks to the many friends and colleagues who helped nourish our vision and cheer us on: Tim Benedict, Ben Benjamin, Scott Bentson, Brian Early, Rob Gilbert, Alan Goldberg, Michael A. Greider, Lyle and Gabe Hanson, Harry Hoopis, Daryl Johnson, Larry LaBelle, Skip Lockwood, Cecile McKenzie, Ed Michalek, Jim Nemec, Tom Peterson, Paul Steffen, John and Shirley Tyler, Peter Vandermark, Sandy Wolf, and Gil Williams. A special thanks to Ron Young, who provided invaluable support, encouragement and feedback throughout the project.

We especially thank our families for exposing us to just the right blends of confidence and skepticism, encouragement and impatience to keep us on track with this long and difficult project. It's Teresa and Kate (Steve) and Karen and Julia (Pete) who gave up the most to make this book a reality. It's in their eyes, more than anyone else's, that we want to be heroes.

Finally, we thank each other for a collaboration so satisfying that the book itself is frosting on the cake. *Following Through* happened because together we made it happen. We relentlessly helped each other practice what we preach about following through. What we learned about the "art of following through together" would fill volumes.

Steve Levinson and Pete Greider

Contents

Following Through ... from a Different Angle

• Thought-provoking commentary on the trials and
tribulations of good intentions •

Contents

The Leaky Bucket

This is a true story.

Frank carried the bucket to the river to get some water for cooking. When he got back to his campsite, he was surprised to find that the bucket was empty. Apparently it had a huge hole in it. "But I still need water," he thought to himself, "and this bucket's not supposed to leak." So he picked up the bucket and headed for the river again. This time, he made a point of filling the bucket right up to the rim. Then, with considerable optimism, he headed back to the campsite. By the time he arrived, the bucket was empty again. "Oh well," he sighed, "I still need water." So he picked up the bucket and back to the river he went.

Did we say that this is a true story? Well, actually, we did change a minor detail or two to protect "the innocent."

You see, the story is not really about a clueless camper who keeps going to the river to fill a leaky bucket with water. It's about all of us who keep filling our minds with good intentions—great ideas about how to improve our lives. And the story is not really about getting nowhere because we keep counting on a bucket that *should* hold water, but doesn't. It's about getting nowhere because we keep counting on a mind that *should* be designed for follow through, but isn't.

FOLLOWING THROUGH: A NEW PERSPECTIVE

The truth of the matter is that you always know the right thing to do. The hard part is doing it.

—General Norman Schwarzkopf

CHAPTER 1

Poor Follow Through: It's No Laughing Matter

May all your troubles last as long as your New Year's Resolutions.

—Joey Adams

Think about some of the promises you've made to yourself lately—important promises like the ones we heard from the hundreds of people we interviewed for this book:

- "I really love my kids. Of course, you'd never know it if you saw how little time I actually spend with them. All I do is work, work, work. I keep saying I'm going to spend more time with my kids, but I never do. And I feel so guilty about it! From now on, I'm going to spend at least an hour every day with them."
- "This messy office is driving me crazy! I get so discouraged every morning when I walk in and see all the stacks of paper on my desk. Some days, it seems like I spend more time trying to find things than I do actually working. I'm

going to stay late on Thursday night and get this place organized. And then I'm going to keep it that way."

- "I just came back from a great seminar. It was a real eye-opener. I learned that a lot of my unhappiness comes from being so hard on myself. I realized that I have to start giving myself more credit for the things that I do well. And that's exactly what I'm going to do from now on."

- "I've had it with this job! Sure, I'm making good money. But I'm miserable. It's even starting to affect my health and my family life. And it's only going to get worse. It's time to face the music and start sending out resumes."

- There's hardly a minute that goes by that I don't feel awful about my weight. I've tried everything. I'm sure I've been on at least a dozen diets in the last two or three years. I usually lose weight but then I gain it all back. I had just about given up. But now, after reading a great new book about weight loss, I have hope again. I'm going to start exercising tomorrow—and no more junk food either!"

- "There are so many worthwhile things I could be doing after dinner instead of watching TV—playing with the kids, working on my quilts, reading a good mystery— you name it! But almost every night, sitting down to watch 'just one show' turns into a wasted evening. It's ridiculous! From now on, I'm going to make sure I get involved in something worthwhile right after dinner."

- "I finally learned my lesson! My assistant just quit. She's the third one this year. She was an absolute gem. My partner keeps telling me that I'm driving good people away because I'm so critical. It's hard to admit it, but he's right. It's killing me to keep losing good people like this. From now on, I'm going to make sure that my employees always know how much I appreciate them."

Now, answer this question honestly: Of all the promises you've made, how many have you kept?

If you've made more promises than you've kept, you're hardly alone.

Poor follow through—consciously deciding to do something, but then not doing it—is a fact of life. Even when the stakes are high, we humans often fail to act in accord with our own good intentions. We know what we should do. But all too often, we either don't do it at all, or we start out with a bang and then fizzle out long before the job is done.

Yes, there's often a wide gap between intending and doing.

We intend to start our own business, get fit, stick to a budget, learn a new skill, stop procrastinating, or become a better mate, parent, friend, or supervisor. Although we know exactly what we need to do, often we don't do it.

We may joke about it, but our failure to follow through on our intentions is really no laughing matter—not when you consider how much it actually costs us.

For example, just ask the 50 percent of heart attack victims who intend to follow their doctors' recommendations for diet and exercise, but don't; or the 92 percent of enthusiastic weight loss program participants who drop out before they reach their weight loss goal; or the estimated 19,400,000 out of 20,000,000 people who intended to quit smoking last year, but failed.

Poor follow through—failing to keep important promises to ourselves and others—does a lot more than just threaten our health. It takes a toll on virtually every aspect of our lives. It prevents us from achieving personal, financial, and career goals that should be well within our reach. It damages our relationships, produces stress, and creates regrets. It robs us of credibility, self-esteem, and peace of mind. Poor follow through deprives us, our families, our businesses, and our communities of the full benefit of our intelligence, talent, imagination, and hard work.

Clearly, poor follow through is a big problem. Why, then, don't we take it more seriously?

That's a good question. And it's the very question that prompted us to write this book.

Too Much "Wiggle Room"?

Perhaps we don't take poor follow through more seriously because we don't quite appreciate how much it's costing us.

One reason that we underestimate the cost of poor follow through is that we usually don't get the "bill" for our follow through failures until long after we've failed. We're on the "fail now, pay later" plan.

For example, what happens if you fail to follow through on your intention to spend more time with your kids? Although you're likely to pay dearly later on, failing may not cost you a thing today. The same is true for failing to quit smoking, failing to stick to a low-fat diet, or failing to address a problem you have with your mate or your boss.

We can break promise after promise without incurring any obvious costs right now. It's only when we've already gone too far down the road—for example, after experiencing a divorce, a heart attack, a missed promotion, or a troubled teenager—that we begin to grasp just how much poor follow through has cost us.

Another reason that we don't realize how much poor follow through is costing us is that the connection between failing to follow through and getting bad results isn't an absolutely air-tight one. There's some "wiggle room."

For example, suppose we ignore all our good intentions— we smoke two packs a day, drink too much, and eat all the wrong foods. We might well end up paying dearly for our negligence by getting sick and dying young. But then again, we might not. We might instead be lucky enough to live to be a hundred. On the other hand, we could follow through perfectly on our intentions—exercise regularly, eat right, and get regular checkups. We might well end up being rewarded for our diligence by enjoying years of good health and living to a ripe old age. But then again, we might not. We might instead have a heart attack and drop dead in our prime.

Just knowing that we might not have to pay anything at all for our follow through failures allows us to take poor follow through less seriously than we should. And so does knowing that following through perfectly doesn't guarantee good results.

What if there was no wiggle room? What if we knew for sure that we would get a "bill" for every single one of our follow through failures? What's more, what if we knew that the bill would always come immediately?

It would be an entirely different ball game if, for example, we knew that smoking just one cigarette would kill us; that ignoring a child just once would cause immediate and permanent harm; or that failing to tackle a problem at work today would end your career today? The very thought of failing to follow through would indeed be alarming.

Business As Usual

Perhaps the biggest reason that we don't take poor follow through more seriously is that we're just plain used to it! Poor follow through is a fixture in our lives. It's business as usual. It's like water to a fish. Because it's everywhere, we just don't notice it. It just doesn't stand out.

Poor follow through is more like a very slow leak than a sudden explosion. And even though it's the slow leaks that may ultimately do us the most harm, we humans are wired to take explosions more seriously.

Car accidents and crimes—even minor fender benders and petty thefts—are like explosions. They get our attention. They engage our emotions. They mobilize us. They urge us to take action. In contrast, follow through failures—no matter how much they can actually harm us—only make us yawn.

Unfortunately, when we as individuals yawn, so does society. Even though poor follow through undoubtedly claims more victims than do all the car accidents, name-brand diseases, and crimes combined, society more or less ignores the problem. Instead of placing poor follow through in the category of "serious problems that demand a solution," society looks the other way.

Poor follow through would indeed get the attention it deserves if our follow through failures were more like car accidents. If follow through failures happened infrequently enough to stand out, and if the damage they did was immediate and definite, they'd get our attention. They'd engage our emotions. They'd urge us individually and collectively to take action.

But, unfortunately, that's not the way it is. And so we're oblivious when we really should be alarmed.

Looking in All the Wrong Places

Being oblivious prevents us from solving the problem of poor follow through. It means making the same mistakes over and over and over again. It means just "assuming" that we'll follow through "next time" instead of actually doing something to make follow through a reality.

In a sense, we're like the inebriated fellow who searched for his keys under the streetlight because it was too dark to search where he dropped them. We don't seem to get it! We keep reacting to our follow through failures by looking for the solution in the wrong place. We assume that all we need to succeed "next time" is more advice, a different approach, or the perfect program. And so we reach for another seminar, book, tape, or motivational speaker—another intoxicating dose of new ideas about what we should do to achieve our goals. And in our excitement, we overlook the obvious:

We don't have a problem knowing what we should do. The problem is that we just don't do it!

Why We Wrote This Book

We're convinced that poor follow through is a big problem and that it deserves to be taken far more seriously than it is. We believe that it's about time we found out what really causes poor follow through.

And it's about time we learned how to overcome it.

That's why we spent the last several years shining a spotlight into the dark hole in inner space where our good intentions disappear. And that's why we're so eager to tell you about the startling discoveries we made.

We uncovered a fundamental truth about the human mind— a basic fact that's ignored by the myriad of self-improvement experts and programs that invite us in, excite our hopes, and then leave us flat. We found out why we humans so often get nothing but disappointment in return for the sizable investment we make in self-improvement; why we so often allow our very best goals and plans to get lost in the shuffle and fade away; why we always seem to have more wisdom than we use.

We learned that, contrary to conventional wisdom, poor follow through is not caused primarily by a lack of willpower, insufficient motivation, low self-esteem, fear of success, or deep, dark character defects. We learned that poor follow through is not our fault! It's caused, amazingly, by the paradoxical way the human mind is designed.

We discovered that although the mind is beautifully designed to produce intentions capable of guiding us effectively through life, the mind has a design flaw that robs intentions of the power they deserve and, in the process, deprives us of the benefit of our intentions. Surprisingly, the mind has no built-in way to keep intentions—no matter how important they are—in the driver's seat. The ironic result is that the very same mind that produces intentions often fails to take them seriously.

Fortunately, by studying the mixed-up way the mind treats intentions, we learned more than just why humans keep dropping the ball. We discovered what it takes to follow through despite the mind's design problems.

No More Crossed Fingers

The mission of *Following Through* is to change forever the way you experience and treat your own good intentions.

In the following chapters, we'll introduce you to an entirely new approach to following through. We'll show you how our discovery of what's wrong with the human mind gives rise to a simple, step-by-step method for following through on virtually any intention.

You'll learn, for example, how to orchestrate outside influences to keep you moving towards inner-directed goals; how to use "leverage" to get the biggest bang out of every motivational "buck"; and how to create "cues" to keep your mind automatically locked in on a good intention until you achieve your goal.

Most of all, you'll learn that following through means more than keeping your fingers crossed and hoping for the best. It means taking the bull by the horns—deliberately taking action to make sure you'll follow through. Equipped with a fresh perspective, some exciting new concepts, and a toolbox full of bold new follow through strategies, you'll be ready to do just that.

Following Through is dedicated to helping you do a better

job of keeping your promises—both big and small—from now on. From turbocharging your career to improving your health, your relationships, or your financial condition to just getting your taxes done early this year, *Following Through* will show you how to transform your good *intentions* into good *results*.

The Unreliable "Iwanit" Button

Sporge is an experienced intergalactic anthropologist. We asked her to share her observations on how the inhabitants of various planets follow through.

"Let me start with my favorite planet. It's called Sureandeasy. On Sureandeasy all you have to do to get whatever you want is push the 'Iwanit' button. The button is easy to push and it always works. So, for Sureandeaseans, following through is no problem at all. All you have to do is decide what you want, push the 'Iwanit' button, and presto, you get it! Not surprisingly, Sureandeaseans have a *perfect* record of following through.

"Then there's my second favorite planet, Hardbutsure. Life on Hardbutsure is a lot like it is on Sureandeasy, but with one important difference. To get what you want on Hardbutsure, not only do you have to push the 'Iwanit' button, you have to push it really, really hard and hold it for a long, long time. Except for the rare Hardbutsurean who gets tired of pushing the button and gives up too soon, Hardbutsureans do an excellent job of following through. That's because they learn early on in life that working hard and being persistent *always* pays off."

"Sporge," we asked, "on which planet is follow through the biggest problem?"

"That's easy," she said. "The answer is Planet Earth. Follow through is a big, big problem for Earthlings. The reason is, on Earth, you can never predict how the 'Iwanit' button is going to work. Sometimes you can push it with all your might, and keep on pushing it for a long, long time, and still nothing happens. Then someone can come along, barely touch the button, and, bingo, instantly get exactly what they want. I'll tell you, life is confusing for Earthlings. There are just no hard and fast rules on Earth about how hard and how long you have to work to get what you want.

"For example, I once met an Earthling named Dale who had put his heart and soul into making his business successful. He worked long, hard hours every day and made one sacrifice after another in an effort to achieve the success he so desperately wanted. Well, despite his hard work and persistence, his business failed. Dale lost just about everything. His neighbor, who wanted success just as badly as Dale did, put forth very little effort to achieve it. He took only easy jobs and would keep them only as long as they stayed easy. Well, Dale's neighbor won a huge sum of money in a lottery! I remember wondering what Dale must have been thinking as his neighbor waved goodbye and drove off in the new car that Dale had always wanted to the kind of new home that Dale had always dreamed of.

"Then there was the Earthling I knew who worked really hard at staying healthy. She ate right, got plenty of exercise, took vitamins, and always followed doctors' orders. She got cancer and died young. Her neighbor invested no effort at all in staying healthy, although she certainly preferred health to sickness. She smoked cigarettes, ate all the wrong foods, never went for checkups, and got as little exercise as possible. She ended up living a long and healthy life.

"Earthlings aren't stupid. Like Sureandeaseans and Hardbutsureans, Earthlings pay close attention to how the 'Iwanit' button works for themselves and their neighbors. And they learn—or at least they try to learn—from what they see.

"What most Earthlings see, of course, is that there are no guarantees that hard work and persistence will pay off; that there are no guarantees that the absence of hard work and persistence will hurt. So, many Earthlings learn to give up if they don't get results quickly. And some even learn not to try at all.

"When you think about it, it's really no wonder that Earthlings have the worst record of follow through in the Universe."

CHAPTER 2

The Follow Through Fairy Tale

Nothing is as fatiguing as the continued hanging on of an uncompleted task.

—William James

Are you ready to tackle the problem of poor follow through? If you realize how much you have to lose by ignoring the problem, and how much you have to gain by overcoming it, then you're ready to take the first step.

The first step is to take your head out of the clouds.

We humans have to scrap our fairy tale notions about how good intentions work. We think we understand what it takes to follow through, but frankly, we're dead wrong. And because we're wrong, we keep making the same mistake over and over and over again.

Without even realizing it, we assume that just having an intention—making a decision about what we're going to do—is all it takes to follow through. We think that good intentions are like products that come with "everything included"—

everything we need to follow through. We call this way of thinking the Follow Through Fairy Tale.

In fairy tales, wishes magically come true. In the Follow Through Fairy Tale, good intentions magically produce good results. Dr. Seuss nicely illustrated the Follow Through Fairy Tale when he wrote:

> *You have brains in your head*
> *You have feet in your shoes*
> *You can steer yourself*
> *Any direction you choose.*

The Follow Through Fairy Tale is irresistibly appealing. It makes perfectly good sense. "Steering"—using "the brains in your head" to decide what to do—is all it takes! What more could you need? Just decide to eat more healthily, read a book every month, or change a bad attitude, and you'll automatically do it. It's as simple as that!

The Follow Through Fairy Tale is appealing and logical. But there's only one problem: It's a fairy tale!

The truth, Dr. Seuss, is that

> *We have brains in our head*
> *We have feet in our shoes*
> *But between "steering" and "doing"*
> *There's a whole lot we lose!*

The "brains in our head" are just not connected as well as we'd like to think they are to the "feet in our shoes." We steer, alright. But our intentions don't always control our actions. Often we steer one way, and we behave another. And yet, we keep on steering as if steering is all it takes.

Why? Because it just *seems* that good intentions should produce good results.

The Strong Grip of the Follow Through Fairy Tale

It's irresistibly logical: *Intending* should mean *doing*—especially when our intentions are truly important.

How could anything make more sense? When what we've decided to do stands to improve our life, or the lives of our loved ones, or maybe even prevent a catastrophe, of course we'll follow through! There'd be something wrong with us if we didn't.

That's exactly what Greg thought.

My accident made me realize that although my kids are more important to me than anything else, I hadn't been acting that way. I put them off all the time, made them feel as if they were interfering with something more important, and did a lousy job of keeping the promises I made to them. It was painful to see the truth. But I faced it. I decided that from that point on, I would always treat my kids as the most important people in my life because that's exactly what they are. From then on, my kids would always come first.

Although I made good on my promise for a while, it didn't take long before I started to slip. And before I knew it, I was completely back to my old ways. When I realized what had happened, I was so disgusted with myself. I felt so guilty.

Like most of the people we interviewed, Greg, without realizing it, believed in the Follow Through Fairy Tale. He subscribed to the popular belief that "If it's really important, I'll do it for sure." He assumed that since his intention to spend more time with his kids was so important, he would definitely follow through. In other words, he expected his good intention to work the way it *should* have worked instead of the way it really did work.

It's no wonder, then, that when Greg didn't follow through, he blamed himself for not caring enough. "I'm just not the kind of father I should be," he thought. "I don't know what's wrong with me."

Sam was another casualty of the Follow Through Fairy Tale. And for Sam, the stakes were sky high. His life depended on following through.

After his heart attack, Sam just assumed he would follow through on his intention to change his living habits. There was no doubt in his mind about how important it was. He knew better than most people because Sam was a doctor. He had treated hundreds of patients who had suffered heart attacks. And he'd seen lots of them die. Yet within just a few months of his heart attack, Sam slacked off on his exercise program, his low-fat diet, and his resolve to spend more relaxing time with his family.

"I don't get it," Sam told us as he struggled to make sense of his failure. "I know exactly what I have to do. I realize that it's a matter of life and death. And I definitely prefer the former to the latter. It just doesn't make any sense to me."

Failing to follow through on a "life and death" intention didn't make sense to Carolyn either. A highly respected, strong-willed professor, Carolyn is one of hundreds of thousands of people who are convinced they should quit smoking, but don't. What's more, she watched her own father die a horrible death from lung cancer. "I think of myself as a pretty intelligent person," she told us. "But this is unbelievably stupid."

That's right, Professor. Our good intentions don't work the way we think they should. And that's right, Doctor. It makes no sense at all.

Seeking Solid Ground

It's perplexing that our good intentions don't work the way we expect them to work. Especially when our intentions are extremely important, it really is surprising that we don't follow through every time. Surely, though, we must be on solid ground in thinking that enthusiasm will guarantee good results. When we're so excited that we can "hardly wait" to act on an intention, we'll follow through for sure. Right?

That's certainly what Dan thought.

Dan is a seasoned salesperson who eagerly joins the millions of businesspeople each year who attend seminars, training programs, and conventions in search of new ways to advance their careers and improve productivity and job satisfaction. Over the past ten years, Dan figures he's been exposed to hundreds of exciting new ideas.

We could feel Dan's enthusiasm build as he described some of the ideas he picked up at a conference in Atlanta last summer. "This speaker really knew his stuff," Dan told us. "I remember I kept thinking, 'these ideas are incredible.' I felt like there was electricity running through me. I knew that if I went home and applied even half of what this guy was suggesting, my career would really take off."

Dan left the conference feeling inspired. He was convinced that he had found the missing ingredient that would set his career on fire. "I was so excited," he told us, "I could hardly wait to get back to work and start using what I had learned."

Dan recalled that it was about three weeks later when, while searching through his briefcase for a file, he came across his five pages of "great ideas" from the Atlanta conference. "Oh, my God," he gasped. "Look at this stuff. I forgot all about it! If I had used this with Smith yesterday, I would have made the sale for sure." He recalled thinking about it in the car all the way home that night. "I can't believe I haven't followed through on any of that speaker's ideas! What a fool I am!" he thought.

Dan confessed that this was certainly not the only time he had blown it. In fact, going ahead and actually implementing an exciting idea was clearly the exception rather than the rule. "I don't get it," Dan told us. "I'm really serious about my career. I just assume that if I come across a great practical idea, I'll put it into practice. Why wouldn't I?" The only thing that made Dan feel a little better about his own follow through failures was the realization that he was in good company. "Hey, I'm not the only one, you know," he told us. "You should see the other guys in my department. Heck, you should see my boss!"

Marie experienced the same kind of puzzling failure to transform enthusiasm into action, only for Marie it occurred in her personal life rather than in her career.

Marie was troubled by the amount of arguing she and her husband did. It seemed they just couldn't stop pressing each other's hot buttons. Then she came across a down-to-earth article entitled "Six Steps to Defusing Arguments." The author's suggestions struck Marie as being fresh, practical, and right on target. She remembered thinking as she finished the article, "I can't wait to try out these ideas."

When we talked to her three months later, Marie was still waiting. "I really wanted to improve my marriage," she said. "And I was really excited about the suggestions in the article. I don't know why I didn't follow through. I don't understand it."

Well, at least Marie read the entire article. When it comes to reading, most of us start a lot more articles and books than we actually finish.

According to some estimates, 90 percent of the books purchased in bookstores never get read past the first chapter. Surely, people wouldn't spend their hard-earned money on these books unless they were enthusiastic about reading them. So why does "I-gotta-have-it" turn so quickly into "I'll-finish-it-someday"? And how come "someday" hardly ever comes?

And speaking of books, when we ran into Scott, he had just purchased the latest "breakthrough" diet book. To say he was excited would be an understatement. When we asked him if he thought he would follow through, Scott could barely contain his enthusiasm. "You bet I will. Why wouldn't I? I'm overweight. I've got a lot of health problems in my family. And besides, I learned about this new diet on TV. It's a miracle. It really sounds terrific."

Scott went on to tell us that over the years he had purchased at least twenty miracle diet books. Unfortunately, he hadn't yet had a single miracle in his own life. Of course, he acknowledged, neither had he actually followed any of the diets for very long. In fact, he admitted, "I've never actually finished reading any of the diet books." Still, Scott was confident that "this time" he'd follow through. Why wouldn't he?

Scott's unfounded optimism about following through was echoed by Patty, who had just paid for her third health club membership. She had signed up twice before, but both times stopped working out within just a few weeks of joining. She just *knew* she'd follow through "this time." She loved the new health club and was really looking forward to getting fit. So with absolutely no hesitation, Patty once again paid a sizable nonrefundable deposit.

When we spoke with Patty several weeks later, she was perplexed. She had fizzled out again! She felt only a little less troubled by her failure when she learned that she was in good company. According to an anonymous spokesperson for one popular health club, nearly three out of four new members stop going within just three months of signing up.

Dan, Marie, Scott, and Patty were all puzzled by their failures because they believed in the Follow Through Fairy Tale. They just assumed that because they were so enthusiastic about their intentions, they would follow through for sure. They were surprised that when it came time for the "rubber" to meet the road, there was no rubber left! Why, they wondered, after starting out with so much inspiration and optimism, did they end up with such poor results?

The answer is perplexing and disappointing, but really quite simple: Our good intentions don't work the way we think they should. Not even enthusiasm will guarantee good results.

"Easy" Does It, Right?

Surely we must be right in assuming that we'll follow through when it's easy. If it's really a cinch to do what we intend to do, of course we'll follow through, won't we?

That's certainly what Gloria thought.

Gloria is sold on vitamins. She's absolutely convinced that taking vitamins regularly will keep her healthy. All she has to do is take one vitamin a day. No big deal, right? What could be easier? A few seconds out of her life once a day is all it takes.

So how come Gloria fails to take her vitamins almost half the time? It's not that she forgets. She thinks about it every time she sees the bottle on the counter. And it's not because she's changed her mind about how important it is for her to take vitamins. She's just as convinced as she was when she ordered "a year's supply." Nothing's changed. She just doesn't follow through.

"It's ridiculous!" Gloria told us. "I know I'm not accomplishing anything unless I take my vitamins every single day. It's so easy to do it. It just doesn't make any sense not to."

Failing to follow through when following through *should* be so easy didn't make any sense to Kyle either.

Kyle figured that it should be a piece of cake to stop biting his nails. He was certainly motivated. There were lots of good reasons for him to do it. His bitten nails looked terrible and sometimes, when he bit them down too far, it was actually painful.

No wonder Kyle's so frustrated that he's still biting. "I don't get it," he told us. "How could anything be easier?"

Nancy's another frustrated member of the "But It Should Be So Easy" Club. She's a talented college golfer who's highly motivated to play well. According to her coach, all Nancy has to do to improve her performance dramatically is to keep her head down and her eye on the ball. Easy enough, right? It should be a cinch, Nancy figured, especially since she needs no convincing. She already knows how much better she plays when she follows her coach's advice.

Some cinch! The last time her coach counted, Nancy had kept her head down and her eye on the ball less than 30 percent of the time!

How come, instead of doing what she's decided to do, Nancy keeps lifting her head before striking the ball? "I have no idea," she told us. "I'm so disgusted with myself."

Nancy, Kyle, and Gloria all thought they were on solid ground in assuming that they'd follow through. After all, what could be easier than taking a vitamin, not biting your nails, or keeping your eye on a stationary golf ball? Yet, for all three, what looked like solid ground turned out to be quicksand.

So, when it comes to following through, *easy* doesn't do it either.

Time to Move On

The bottom line is that as long as we continue to expect our intentions to work the way they *should* instead of the way they *do*, we'll just keep making the same mistakes over and over again. We'll get absolutely nowhere but frustrated.

Fairy tales are great. But when believing in them prevents us from doing everything we can to improve our lives, it's time to move on. So it is with the Follow Through Fairy Tale. It's time for us to face the truth about how our good intentions work.

No matter how important, exciting, or easy they are, our good intentions *don't* magically lead to good results. The truth is disappointing. The truth is perplexing. But the truth is the truth.

Discarding the Follow Through Fairy Tale is the first step in solving the problem of poor follow through.

And a giant step it is.

The Fizz That Fizzles

If truth in advertising were ever to become a reality, the "Self-Improvement" section of your neighborhood bookstore would have to be renamed the "Wishful Thinking" section. Most of the books you find there are dripping wet with wishful thinking. They ooze irresistibly appealing humanistic notions. The results they promise give you goose bumps. They excite and inspire and motivate.

Unfortunately, however, these books typically tell us more about what we'd like to believe about ourselves than about what's really true. They treat us like bottled soda. They shake us up and build our excitement. Then, following a glorious but decidedly short-lived effervescence, we fizzle out and go flat.

Then we just go back for more.

CHAPTER 3

The Ever-Popular "It Must Be Me" Theory

We want the facts to fit the preconceptions.
When they don't, it is easier to ignore the facts
than to change the preconceptions.

—Jessamyn West

It's human nature to insist on making sense of things. We continuously strive to understand ourselves and the world around us. We're so eager to know how things work that, long before all the facts are in, we construct theories to explain what's happening.

Scientists aren't the only ones who build theories. We all build them, although often without realizing it. Our theories are shaped by our own observations, by what we learn from others, and by our culture. We build each theory on a foundation of assumptions—what we think is true.

Of course, a theory doesn't have to be accurate to work. All it has to do is enable us to make sense of what we experience. We'll hang on to a theory as long as it leaves us convinced that we "know"—even if what we "know" is actually way off the mark. In fact, it's not unusual for even the most popular theories to be wrong. For example, long before we "knew" that the world was round, we "knew" that it was flat.

A Theory Built on a Shaky Foundation

In trying to make sense of poor follow through, most people accept a theory that *seems* to explain what's happening. We call the theory the *It Must Be Me* theory.

The theory goes something like this: It's *you* who determines whether or not you'll follow through. Your follow through "record," therefore, is a straightforward expression of your character. It reveals how motivated you are, how much self-discipline and willpower you have. According to the *It Must Be Me* theory, follow through is, more or less, a character trait. The more of the "follow through trait" you have, the better you'll follow through. The less of it you have, the worse you'll follow through. It's as simple as that.

In many respects, the *It Must Be Me* theory works well. It seems to do a good job of explaining why people follow through and why they don't. We all know people who seem to follow through on *everything*. And we all know people who seem to follow through on *nothing*. Follow through *must be* a character trait. What else could it be?

But there's a problem with the *It Must Be Me* theory—and it's a whopper. The theory, instead of being built on a solid foundation of facts, is built on a fairy tale. It rests on the sadly incorrect assumption that our good intentions will work the way they *should;* that if it's important enough, exciting enough, or easy enough, we'll follow through for sure. As the Follow Through Fairy Tale goes, "Good intentions magically produce good results."

It Must Be My Fault

The *It Must Be Me* theory has done a number on us. It's caused us to view, experience, and react to poor follow through in a way that makes us feel unnecessarily guilty.

If good intentions are supposed to magically produce good results, then bad results can only mean one thing: "You screwed up." That's right. The *It Must Be Me* theory puts the blame for follow through failures squarely on your shoulders.

Accepting the theory means that whenever you fail to follow through on a good intention, you'll shake your finger at yourself and ask, "Hey, what's wrong with me?" And your answer will probably go something like this: "I guess I just don't have enough motivation, self-discipline, or willpower." You figure, in other words, that following through is purely and simply a matter of character. You never for a moment consider the possibility that there could be another explanation.

The Theory Goes One Way, the Facts Go Another

The *It Must Be Me* theory leaves us thinking that we know why we fail to follow through. But what we "know" just doesn't square with the facts. The theory leaves us with a blind spot that prevents us from seeing what's really going on.

The fact is, follow through is *not* simply a matter of character.

Although there are indeed those people out there who follow through on just about everything and those who follow through on very little, most of us have decidedly mixed records. Sometimes we follow through and sometimes we don't. For most of us, following through is hardly an across-the-board phenomenon.

The truth is, follow through is more a matter of *circumstances* than it is a matter of *character*. How well we follow through, we discovered, depends less on who we are than it does on the particular thing we intend to do and what's going on around us.

Look at Hank, for example.

Hank has lower back pain. Although he's intended for years to do back exercises that should help, he's never followed through. Neither has he followed through on the "Never again!" promise he makes to himself every year as he speeds to the post office with his tax return at the very last minute. Ditto for his intentions to spend more time playing with his seven-year-old daughter, to fix the bathroom faucet which has been leaking since 1993, or to quit smoking despite his doctor's repeated warnings and his own serious worries about his health.

Hank is living proof of the *It Must Be Me* theory of poor follow through. Or is he?

Seven times a year, Hank drives three hours in heavy traffic each way, pays over two hundred dollars, and sits outside, often in dreadful weather, for hours. Yet Hank still follows through every time. "A team of wild horses couldn't stop me," he told us matter-of-factly.

Stop him from what?

From attending all of the Green Bay Packers home games.

You see, Hank is a sports fan. And, like millions of sports fans, he follows through perfectly—when it comes to sports, that is. He never "forgets" to check the scores in the morning paper. He arrives at the stadium an hour early for home games, and he turns the TV on in plenty of time for the pregame show when his team is on the road. And he's never "too busy" to place his bet in the office pool on Fridays.

Yes, despite substantial financial, emotional, and physical obstacles, Hank has an unblemished record of following through with the Packers, every week, every season, for years and years.

If you insist on hanging on to the *It Must Be Me* theory,

you could easily say that Hank is the kind of person who will put himself out as long as there's fun to be had. Otherwise, he's just plain lazy. You *could* say that. But it wouldn't be true.

You see, Hank always follows through on his intentions to take the garbage out on time (even though he absolutely hates doing it), to walk the dog (even when it means missing a chunk of his favorite TV show), and to make sure his diabetic daughter gets her insulin shots regularly (even though he dreads doing it).

Although we assume it's right because it just seems right, the *It Must Be Me* theory is way off the mark. It doesn't account for why people follow through on some intentions and not on others. It can't explain Hank's mixed follow through record. Neither can it explain Jay's.

Jay is a busy, productive, and highly respected professional. In addition to his day job, he runs a successful business; he teaches; he does volunteer work; he sits on various boards and committees. A true pillar of the community, Jay's promises are as good as gold. He oozes motivation, self-discipline, and willpower. Talk about follow through!

But watch Jay closely as he finishes up a tedious word-processing project in his home office. As he gets to the very last of the thirty or so business letters he has to write, he notices that the zip code for one address is missing. No problem. Jay has a zip code directory, which is sitting right where his wife put it—on the bookcase next to his desk. He reaches for the directory, finds the missing zip code, and types it in. There. He's done.

Before he gets up, Jay hears a little voice in his mind say, "Put the directory back where it belongs so that you won't have to hunt for it when you need it next." Putting it back would certainly be the right thing to do. It would take no time at all, and it would require a minuscule amount of effort—

not much effort at all for someone who once spent hundreds of torturous hours working on a doctoral dissertation.

But Jay ignores the intelligent little voice—he ignores the good intention. He leaves the zip code directory right where he set it down—in the midst of the incredible mess on his desk. He *knows* that there's a good chance that by the next time he needs the zip code directory, it will have been swallowed whole by the mess. He *knows* he'll be frustrated. He *knows* the papers will fly as he swears and fusses and fumes his way through the many piles in search of "that damned zip code directory." How does he know? Jay, the follow through dynamo, has been there many times before.

Discovering the Power of Circumstances

When it comes to follow through, Hank and Jay range from unstoppable speeding bullets to sea slugs. How well they follow through depends on the particular thing they intend to do and on the situation they're in. So what happened to the all-important follow through trait?

The answer, of course, is that the *It Must Be Me* theory grossly exaggerates the role that character plays in follow through. Accepting the theory is like wearing a special pair of glasses that focuses your attention on *character* and blinds you to the powerful effect that other factors have on follow through. Take off the glasses, and the power of *circumstances* will jump right out at you.

Sarah, for example, is chronically late for everything—everything except planes, that is. Even when there are major obstacles in her way, including traffic, bad weather, and all the little hassles that accompany getting ready for a trip, she always makes it to the airport on time. Something causes her to suddenly change her ways, as if by magic, when she has a plane to catch.

And speaking of sudden changes, consider Matt. Like many teenagers, Matt had elevated poor follow through to an art form. As his mother used to say, "Matt makes more promises than a hen lays eggs." So why did Matt suddenly become a veritable master of follow through the minute he stepped off the bus at Parris Island, South Carolina, on his first day of Marine Corps Basic Training?

Athletes of all ages, sizes, personalities, and levels of ability follow through every day. Most of them show up for practice on time and do what their coaches and trainers tell them to do—no matter how difficult or unpleasant it may be. And they don't just do it, they do it with enthusiasm. Yet many of these very same athletes do an awful job of following through on the simplest of intentions in school, with friends, and at home.

Time for a New Theory

Yes, it's time to scrap the troublesome *It Must Be Me* theory. Not only does it unfairly blame us as individuals for our follow through failures, it prevents us from understanding how our good intentions really do work. So instead of learning from our follow through successes and failures, we just keep making the same mistakes over and over and over again.

So let's place the *It Must Be Me* theory where it belongs— on the shelf right next to the *The World Is Flat* theory. It's time to move on.

In the next chapter, we'll set the stage for a new theory of follow through. Unlike the *It Must Be Me* theory, which is based on a fairy tale notion of how our good intentions *should* work, the new theory of follow through is based on the truth about how our good intentions really do work. It rests on our discovery that poor follow through is caused by a design flaw in the human mind. But don't worry. Although it may start off with bad news, the new theory points us in the direction of a delicious opportunity: By understanding rather than ignoring what's wrong with the human mind, we can turn a liability into an asset. With a little creativity, we can actually use the mind's design problems to make our good intentions work better than they ever have before.

CHAPTER 4

In Search of the Real Culprit

Still round the corner there may wait,
A new road or a secret gate.

—J.R.R.Tolkien

So now you know the truth. You've been taking a bum rap for years. Poor follow through isn't your fault.

So whose fault is it?

Rather than just tell you, we're going to show you how we tracked the culprit down and caught "him" red-handed.

It wasn't easy. We had to overcome the worst kind of obstacles—our own assumptions.

You see, when we first set out to find out why people don't follow through, we too were under the influence of the *It Must Be Me* theory. We had our minds set on finding the "follow through trait."

We spoke to hundreds of people about the fate of their intentions. We had no trouble at all finding lots of "evidence" that follow through is a character trait. The only problem was, the evidence was bogus. Instead of being based on facts, the evidence was a product of circular reasoning. It went something like this: "The reason that Mary didn't follow through is that she doesn't have enough willpower. How do we know? Well, *obviously* if Mary *did* have enough willpower, she would have followed through!"

As hard as we tried, we could find no *real* evidence that a follow through trait alone could be responsible for the mixed follow through records of most of the people we interviewed. Willpower, motivation, self-discipline, and strength of character may have been part of the picture, but clearly there was something missing. There had to be more.

Trying Out a Fresh Perspective

We decided that we had been barking up the wrong tree. It was time, we figured, to start from scratch. So we scrapped our assumptions and adopted a fresh approach. We decided to analyze follow through failures the way highway safety experts analyze accidents.

Our logic went something like this: When we intend to do something, we *expect* to follow through. In other words, we expect to go from Point A, *intention,* to Point B, *action.* Therefore, if we don't follow through, why not look at the failure as an "accident" or a "mishap" and try to figure out exactly what caused it?

As we tried out our new perspective, we noticed an interesting difference between the way people try to make sense of car accidents and the way they try to make sense of follow through failures.

When safety experts try to figure out what caused an accident, they don't just consider the driver. They also consider the equipment. They routinely ask, "Is there something about the design of the car itself that could have contributed to this accident?" Perhaps, for example, there's a poorly placed rear-view mirror that obscured the driver's view, or a design flaw in the steering system that caused the driver to lose control.

In contrast, when people try to figure out what causes follow through accidents, they *never* consider the possibility that the design of the equipment—in this case, the human mind—could be to blame.

We were intrigued. Clearly, we humans have a blind spot. We completely overlook the possibility that our follow through accidents could be caused by the way the mind is designed.

The Case of the Invisible Mind

When we explored the blind spot, we were surprised to find that it was quite a bit larger than it first appeared. We learned that we humans are not only blind to the possibility that the mind could cause follow through failures, we're blind to the mind, period! In a sense, the mind is invisible.

As we thought about it, we realized why. We humans are just too close to the mind to experience it as "equipment." The mind is in a class by itself. We experience it in an entirely unique way. It's not like the heart, for example. You can easily stand back from your heart and experience it as equipment. Your heart is part of you, but it's not you. So if your heart fails, you don't automatically consider yourself a failure.

It's hard to stand back from your mind and experience it as a piece of equipment. You and your mind are inseparable. In a sense, you *are* your mind. That's what makes your mind invisible. And that's why you accept total responsibility for what your mind does. So instead of "My mind forgot to turn off the lights," you think, "I forgot to turn off the lights." And instead of "My mind failed to transform a good intention into action," you think, "I screwed up."

Scientists Have Blind Spots Too

We were beginning to understand why people completely overlook the possibility that there could be something wrong with the way the human mind is designed. We were still puzzled, though, by the fact that scientists who devote their time, energy, and talent to studying the mind also overlook this possibility.

We wondered if the scientific community might be suffering from a case of infatuation. After all, the human mind has truly awesome capabilities. It would be easy to get carried away with all the amazing things the mind does and, in the process, overlook the possibility that the mind—just like other pieces of human equipment—isn't designed perfectly.

Scientists certainly don't assume that the human body is perfectly designed. They have no problem, for example, criticizing the design of the human back—blaming it for making people so susceptible to injuries. And they have no problem regarding the appendix as an entirely unnecessary and potentially troublesome part of the digestive system.

The human mind is a product of the very same biological forces that shaped the body. The mind, therefore, is just as likely as the body to have design problems. So, if our scientists are reluctant to criticize the design of the human mind, perhaps it's because they're just too in love with the mind to be objective.

Barking Up the Right Tree

We still had nothing more than a hunch—an inkling—that the human mind might actually deserve less confidence than it inspires; that the design of the mind might be responsible for follow through failures. We had no real evidence. All we knew for sure is that *if* the design of the human mind really is the secret culprit, it's been one heck of an easy secret to keep!

Perhaps we were finally ready to bark up the right tree.

In the next chapter, we'll show you how, with the help of a squirrel and the Minnesota Vikings football team, we confirmed our hunch.

CHAPTER 5

We Have Met the Enemy, And He Is Us

The voyage of discovery is not in seeking new landscapes, but in having new eyes.

—Marcel Proust

I (Steve) live in Minnesota. Early every fall, I have fine intentions of getting a huge supply of firewood ready for the long winter. One chilly Sunday afternoon in November, after many weeks of procrastination, I decided that enough was enough. It was definitely time to get the job done, especially since a big snowstorm was on the way. I also wanted to watch the Minnesota Vikings football game on television, but I decided that the firewood must come first.

As I sat on the couch looking out the window at the place in the yard where a winter's worth of cut and neatly stacked firewood should have been, I noticed a squirrel gathering acorns. I thought, "That squirrel is doing the same thing I'm about to do. He's getting ready for winter."

Then I lingered a while longer to think about how lucky I was to be a human. "After all," I thought, "I have intelligence and foresight. I can use my mind to figure out exactly what I should do. All that little squirrel can do is run on instinct. He probably doesn't even have a clue about why he's picking up acorns and storing them away. He just does it."

Then I watched the football game.

Including the entire halftime show.

And the entire postgame show.

And then I decided that since it would soon be dark and it was already snowing, I might as well watch the next game too.

It hit me: The human mind is magnificently designed, but only to help us do half the job.

The whole job is doing whatever it takes to get what we need and want out of life. The first half of the job is figuring out what to do. The second half of the job is doing it.

When it comes to the first half of the job, the human mind really shines. We humans are experts at figuring out what we should do.

For example, there were lots of reasons why putting up firewood for the winter was the right thing for me to do on that Sunday afternoon in November. I wanted to save money on heating; I was convinced it would be good for me to spend some time swinging an ax and working up a sweat; I looked forward to a sense of accomplishment; and I knew that it would be a whole lot easier to do the work before the snow fell than after it arrived.

My mind did a great job of helping me do the first half of the job. It enabled me to figure out the best course of action—to make one tidy decision that took into account a host of needs, wants, and realities: Put up the firewood this afternoon.

But when it came to the second half of the job—going ahead and actually doing what I'd figured out I should do—my mind took a nosedive.

Just ask my wife. Or ask the electric company that sold us lots of electricity for heating that winter. Or ask the squirrel, who did the whole job, while I did only half.

The Ultimate Irony

If we humans are so intelligent, so sophisticated, and so advanced, how come a squirrel can do a better job of following through?

The answer, we figured, must lie in the way our guidance system works.

Every living thing has a guidance system. At its simplest, a guidance system consists of the functions and processes that cause an organism to do whatever it must do to survive and reproduce. Even a single-celled microorganism has a guidance system. It's made up of a few chemically triggered reflexes or switches that steer and propel the little bugger away from danger and towards food.

Most guidance systems, like the squirrel's, operate largely on the basis of preprogramming or instincts. Mr. Squirrel collects acorns for the winter because he's preprogrammed to react automatically to certain environmental conditions by gathering and storing nuts. The mere presence of these conditions triggers the right behavior.

An instinct-based guidance system is simple and reliable. Expose Mr. Squirrel to the right conditions, and he'll start gathering nuts. It will happen every time because he was programmed at the factory to function this way. The knowledge that gathering nuts for the winter is the right thing to do is hardwired into his guidance system.

Having hardwired knowledge means there's no need for

Mr. Squirrel to watch a video on how to prepare for the winter. No need for him to check with the Squirrel FDA before planning his menu. No need for him to send a stamped, self-addressed envelope to Pueblo, Colorado, to request a pamphlet on the best way to store acorns. Mr. Squirrel doesn't have to figure out what to do. The knowledge he needs was installed at the factory.

Automatically knowing what to do is not the only feature of an instinct-based guidance system that distinguishes it from ours. Besides automatically knowing what to do, Mr. Squirrel is automatically motivated to do it. If he *should* collect nuts for the winter, he *will* collect nuts for the winter.

Being hardwired to act means that there's no need for Mr. Squirrel to listen to a motivational speaker or a lecture from his mother-in-law about being a good provider. He doesn't need any inspiring. He's always psyched up to do the right thing.

Mr. Squirrel's guidance system automatically does the whole job. Yes, having an instinct-based guidance system means always automatically knowing what to do and always automatically having the drive to do it. It means always following through.

There's only one drawback to having a guidance system that operates largely on the basis of built-in knowledge and preprogrammed responses: It's not very flexible. It doesn't allow its owners to tailor their behavior precisely to the circumstances they face. And this can sometimes be a real problem.

For example, I once watched Mr. Squirrel's cousin make the mistake of storing nuts in a tree that the power company was about to cut down. I watched the power company survey the area and then paint a yellow stripe on each of the trees in a long row. As soon as workers started to cut down the first of the marked trees, I knew exactly what was up. The squirrel didn't have a clue. Operating on automatic pilot, he continued to fill a pantry that would be gone long before winter.

Living things that are guided primarily by instinct pay a price for the convenience of always knowing what to do and always being motivated to do it. They follow through even when they shouldn't! Yes, the price of hardwired absolute confidence is sometimes automatically doing the wrong thing.

What Makes the Human Guidance System So Special?

Enter the unique and advanced human guidance system. In many respects, it's evolution's crowning achievement. Ironically, we discovered, it's also the source of our follow through woes.

Instead of automatically tripped switches, the human guidance system relies on the richness of thought to analyze conditions, draw from experience, and use logic to figure out exactly what we should do to get what we need and want out of life. It's designed to enable us to do the very best job of any species of matching our actions to the specific conditions we face and the specific objectives we set.

Because we can figure things out, we can survive—even thrive—under an extraordinarily wide range of conditions. We've figured out how to live in extremely hot climates, extremely cold ones, extremely wet, and extremely dry ones. We've figured out how to breathe under water and to explore outer space; to make deserts bloom; to generate electricity to make life easier; to treat and prevent serious illnesses and dramatically prolong life; and to sacrifice now so that later on we can enjoy retirement, send our kids to college, or have enough firewood to stay inexpensively warm during a long and cold Minnesota winter.

But wait, it gets even better! Not only does each of us figure things out individually, our guidance systems are, in a sense, connected to one another. Our societies generate and disseminate tons of guidance for us all to use. Members of our species dedicate themselves to figuring out what we all should and shouldn't eat, what drugs we should and shouldn't take, what we should do to stay healthy and happy, to get rich, to be attractive to members of the opposite sex, to play better tennis or bridge, and to find the most environmentally friendly laundry detergent.

Individually and collectively, we humans generate a never-ending supply of intelligent guidance. We get smarter all the time about how to live. No other species can come close to our ability to use intelligence to decide on the best course of action.

If the human guidance system sounds impressive, it is. There's only one problem: *It wastes much of the intelligent guidance it produces.*

That's right, it wastes it.

The Trouble With the Human Guidance System

You'd assume that a guidance system that's beautifully designed to produce intelligent guidance would also be beautifully designed to use it. That would make sense.

What we discovered, however, is that the human guidance system doesn't make sense. It isn't designed logically.

It draws on the most incredibly advanced capabilities to give us first-rate guidance in the form of good intentions. Then it lets the guidance go to waste by allowing us to ignore it.

Think of a highly skilled physician who draws on a wealth of expertise to give his patient precisely the right advice. Then think of a patient who lets the advice go to waste by failing to follow it. Thanks to the illogical way the human guidance system is designed, we are at once the good physician and the bad patient!

Life would be very different if the human guidance system were designed logically; if we were as good at following intelligent guidance as we are at producing it.

We'd always automatically behave in accord with our intentions. If we decided we *should* do it, we *would* do it.

All you'd have to do, for example, is decide that it's best for you to eat low-calorie, low-fat foods. The case would be closed. You'd automatically love alfalfa sprouts and hate potato chips. If you decided that you should exercise regularly, you'd just do it. You'd not only think, "I really should exercise," you'd automatically *feel* like exercising. If you decided to spend three hours a day working on a book, playing with your kids, painting the den, or putting up firewood, you'd just do it. Nothing would stop you.

What Was Mother Nature Thinking?

Having a guidance system that does only half the job qualifies us for a rather dubious distinction: *We humans are arguably the only living things that don't consistently do what we know is best.* Accompanying our extraordinary capacity to figure out what we should do is a rather perplexing inclination to often do something else instead.

Why in the world, we wondered, would evolution take our species so far down the path of relying on intelligent guidance without going all the way?

CHAPTER 6

No Wonder We Don't Follow Through!

No matter how loud reason shouts her rules of good conduct, the passions shout much louder.

—Erasmus

During a visit to China in the early 1980's, I (Steve) went to a bank to exchange some currency. I watched the teller use a modern electronic calculator to do the math. After writing down the answer on a slip of paper, the teller dashed into the back room to check her answer with an abacus! Although a modern system for performing calculations was up and running, the teller wasn't quite ready to stop relying on the old system.

Could something similar, we wondered, be going on with the human mind?

A New Theory Begins To Emerge

Here's how our thinking went: Evolution has obviously been experimenting with intelligent guidance as a means of making humans uniquely adaptable. Perhaps Mother Nature has hedged her bet. Rather than fully retiring the primitive survival-oriented guidance system that enabled our distant ancestors to detect and react decisively to danger and opportunity, could She have left the primitive system in place "just in case?" And if so, might this primitive guidance system be working at cross-purposes with the modern intelligence-based guidance system?

The more we thought about it, the more sense it made. And the closer we looked, the more evidence we found that not only is the primitive, survival-oriented guidance system still alive and well, it's the source of our follow through problems.

It's no wonder it feels like we're working against ourselves whenever we intend to do something and then don't. We *are* working against ourselves!

We realized that we humans are at a most awkward stage in our evolutionary development. We are, shall we say, "between guidance systems." Along with a spanking new, state-of-the-art Intelligence-Based Guidance System, we have an ancient, outmoded survival-oriented guidance system that evolution hasn't gotten around to unplugging. Both systems are working to control our behavior at the same time. Unfortunately, the two systems have very different ideas about how we should behave. And, like Democrats and Republicans working simultaneously to advance the country's interests, they're not necessarily working together.

The Squeak-Seeking Primitive Guidance System

The Primitive Guidance System—we'll call it the PGS—has a personality that was well-suited to the way we lived long,

long ago when surviving was all that life was about. Vigilant, reactive, and present-oriented, the system was designed to make sure that you detect and respond to the need, want, threat, or opportunity that's most in your face right now.

The PGS has both feet firmly planted in the present moment. It's in the business of detecting and responding not to well-thought-out intentions, but to what's happening right now. When the PGS notices an itch, for example, it urges you to scratch it. When it notices that you're hungry, the PGS urges you to find something to eat. When it notices that you're feeling lonely, the PGS urges you to search for companionship. When it notices that you're bored and restless doing what you're doing, it urges you to stop and do something else instead. When it notices that you're already late for an important meeting, it urges you to hustle. When it notices that you're feeling compassion for someone else, it urges you to help.

The PGS's simple rule of thumb is this:

Listen for squeaks, and grease the squeakiest wheel.

You can feel the Primitive Guidance System do its thing every time you smell cookies baking in the oven and feel like you just can't wait to eat one; or when you hear your baby screaming and drop everything to find out what's wrong; or when you suddenly realize that the bathroom is a mess and your dinner guests are due in just a few minutes.

Of course, being vigilant, reactive, and present-oriented usually takes you in an entirely different direction than intelligent guidance does. The Primitive Guidance System couldn't care less about intelligent guidance. What it does care about—and all it cares about—is squeak. It notices and urges you to respond to your most intense feelings and sensations—the squeakiest wheels.

A physician told us a wonderful story that illustrates what

it means to have these two very different guidance systems working at cross-purposes.

Dr. James had a mole on his left hand. It had been there for months. Although he would often say to himself, "I really should remove this mole," he kept putting it off. One day at the clinic, he found himself with an unexpected block of free time—a perfect opportunity to remove the pesky mole.

As he gathered the instruments and supplies he needed to do the deed, Dr. James gave himself a little speech. "The mole has to go. I'm a doctor. I know what I'm doing. I've removed lots of moles before. This is no big deal."

With his left hand planted firmly on the examining table, Dr. James approached the mole with a scalpel in his right hand. Suddenly, as if it had a mind of its own, his left hand retreated from the scalpel.

Dr. James reports that he spent the next ten or fifteen minutes chasing his left hand around the examining room.

Frustrated and embarrassed, he gave up.

Dr. James used his intelligence to decide that it was in his best interest to remove the mole. He assumed he could do it because it was the right thing to do. So why couldn't he do it?

Dr. James's good intention failed because his Primitive Guidance System gave the grease to the squeakiest wheel, not the smartest wheel. In the contest for control of Dr. James's behavior, the fear of pain—the intense, immediate feeling—overruled the well-thought-out intention to get rid of a potentially troublesome mole. In short, Dr. James's good intention was outsqueaked.

Calling a Spade a Spade

The answer to the question "Why couldn't Dr. James do it?" points us in the direction of a new theory of follow through, which we call the *Design Flaw* theory. Unlike the *It Must Be Me* theory, which is based on how we think the mind *should* work, the *Design Flaw* theory is based on how the mind really does work.

The *Design Flaw* theory goes like this:

(1) We have two guidance systems operating at the same time. Although both systems are designed to steer us in the right direction, the two systems often have very different ideas of what the right direction is. One functions like a learned professor; the other like a shark. The modern system, the Intelligence-Based Guidance System, uses intelligence to figure out the best course of action. It's designed to make sure we behave in accord with our well-thought-out conclusions about what's best for us. In contrast, the Primitive Guidance System is vigilant, reactive, and present-oriented. It's designed to make sure we respond to immediate threat or opportunity.

(2) Each guidance system does its own thing. There's absolutely no cooperation between the two systems—no mechanism in place to make sure they work together for our benefit.

(3) In the contest to control our behavior, the Primitive Guidance System has a distinct advantage: It's more powerful. Whenever the professor and the shark have different ideas of how we should behave (which is often), the shark is more likely to get its way.

The *Design Flaw* theory's bottom line is this: The real reason we fail to follow through is not because we as individuals lack willpower, self-discipline, or character. It's because we as a species have a design flaw that prevents our good intentions—despite their obvious qualifications—from having enough influence to consistently get the job done.

So if you're reading this, Dr. James, perhaps you can take comfort in knowing that there's a simple explanation for why you left the examining room that day with your mole still intact and your pride injured. You made the same mistake that most of us make every day. You assumed that the mind would work the way it *should* instead of the way it *does*. You assumed that, just because it was most qualified, your intelligent guidance would run the show.

The Ultimate Power Struggle

Picture a car that has two steering wheels and two drivers. Although both steering wheels work, the drivers are oblivious to each other. The driver on the left thinks things through, carefully decides on a destination, and then steers the car towards that destination. The driver on the right has absolutely no destination in mind. He just reacts to whatever happens along the way, steering the car towards whatever grabs his attention at the moment.

Can you imagine what it would be like to be a passenger in the backseat of a car like this? Well, you don't have to imagine it. You're already there!

The driver on the left is your Intelligence-Based Guidance System. It steers you towards good health, for example, by steering clear of all those yummy high-fat foods. Meanwhile, the driver on the right, your Primitive Guidance System, makes a sharp turn and heads right for the potato chips in the vending machine you just spotted. Or your Intelligence-Based Guidance System turns and heads for the library so that you can start working on that term paper that's due next month. Meanwhile, the Primitive Guidance System steers you straight ahead to the next TV show.

Being steered down the road of life by two guidance systems with very different personalities makes for an always challenging and often frustrating ride. It means setting the course, then ignoring it, then setting it and ignoring it again, and again, and again.

CHAPTER 7

The Truth Shall Set Us Free

Men stumble over the truth from time to time, but most pick themselves up and hurry off as if nothing happened.
—Winston Churchill

So now what?

Other than relieving some guilt, what good does it do to know the truth about the root cause of poor follow through? If the problem is that the mind is poorly designed, what can we possibly do about it?

Should you just hold off on that next self-improvement project for a few hundred thousand years while evolution gets the bugs worked out?

No way!

Sure, it's disappointing to find out that the mind doesn't work the way we think it should. But rather than hurt us, knowing the truth can only help.

By not knowing the truth—by believing in the Follow Through Fairy Tale—we've placed ourselves at the mercy of the mind's limitations. Without realizing it, we've relied on the mind to do a job it isn't properly designed to do. Relying on the human mind to transform our good intentions into action is like relying on a heavily advertised but poorly designed home security system to protect us from intruders. We assume the "system" is doing the job, but it isn't. And as long as we assume that everything's okay, poor follow through will continue to be a fixture in our lives.

Learning the truth about the mind's limitations opens the door to progress. If we accept the fact that the mind isn't well-designed to transform our intentions into action, then we can finally ask the right question: How can we get the job done despite the mind's limitations?

There's good reason to be optimistic about being able to overcome the mind's limitations. We humans have a distinguished record of finding a way around our limitations once we face them squarely.

For example, we've done a remarkable job of fulfilling our desire to fly. We did it by acknowledging our disappointing limitations, not by ignoring them. We opened the door to progress when we finally recognized that for us, flying isn't a matter of flapping our arms harder, longer, or exactly the right way. The truth is, we humans are just not physically designed to fly.

Had we not come to terms with our limitations, we'd still be standing on hillsides, jumping out of trees and off cliffs, flapping our arms and trying to fly. Accepting the truth is what allowed us to stop asking the wrong question—"How should we flap?"—and start asking the right question—"How can we fly despite our design limitations?" Asking the right question is what made it possible for us eventually to get off the ground.

Finally Asking the Right Question

When it comes to the important job of transforming our intentions into action, we humans are still in the "flapping our arms and trying to fly" stage of development. We assume that the mind is properly designed to get the job done; that if we just "try harder," we'll follow through; that all we need is more willpower, more self-discipline, more character.

Flap. Flap. Flap. Crash!

The *Design Flaw* theory makes it possible for us to get off the ground. It allows us to move beyond the "flapping our arms and trying to fly" stage of problem-solving. It opens the door to progress by redefining the problem of poor follow through. Instead of encouraging us to ask the *wrong* question— "How can I fix what's wrong with me *personally?*"—the new theory encourages us to ask the *right* question—"How can I follow through despite the human mind's design problems?"

The *Design Flaw* theory does more than just explain why we humans do such a lousy job of following through on our good intentions. It gives us some important clues about what we can do to *compensate* for the mixed-up way the human mind is designed. In fact, the theory goes even further than that. It hints at how we can turn a liability into an asset; how we can improve follow through by learning how to benefit from the very same design problems that normally cause poor follow through.

Getting Help From "the Enemy"

We were just about ready to conclude categorically that the PGS is the enemy of good intentions when we met Theresa, a hard-working sales representative. She was frustrated about her failure to get her taxes done early this year. As we thought about Theresa's follow through failure, something occurred to us. The Primitive Guidance System has another side. *Sometimes,* we realized, the PGS actually *helps* us follow through.

We had been so focused on how the PGS worked against Theresa's intention to get her taxes done *early* that we had almost overlooked something important: The PGS actually helped Theresa get her taxes done *on time.*

It was on a Saturday afternoon in early March that Theresa decided it was a perfect time to get her tax return done. "Why wait until the last minute the way I usually do?" she asked herself. "It's ridiculous. Sure I hate doing my taxes. But if I just do them right now, I won't have to worry about it anymore."

So Theresa sat down at her desk and began working on her taxes. "I'll just keep working until I'm done," she insisted.

As she set out to follow through on her intention, however, Theresa's PGS listened for squeaks. It had no trouble finding them. Her PGS noticed that she was hungry, so it sent her off to the kitchen in search of food. Then, only minutes after she had returned to the table, her PGS noticed that she was thirsty, so it sent her back to the kitchen to get a drink.

In the course of just a couple of hours, Theresa's Primitive Guidance System had detected and urged her to respond to dozens of squeaks, including the sound of her favorite TV show in the distance, her neighbor laughing, the growing pain of boredom, and the restlessness she felt as she thought about all the things she'd rather be doing.

After a brutal two-hour struggle, Theresa's good intention had been defeated. It had been outsqueaked. Disgusted, Theresa went to a movie.

Over the course of the next few weeks, Theresa thought about her taxes often, and she felt sick every time she did. But she steered clear of her desk until the day before her taxes were due.

Finally, Cooperation!

Now, with an intense sense of urgency in her gut, there's Theresa at her desk. She feels like she has absolutely no choice—no wiggle room. Her back is to the wall. "I've just got to do it," she tells herself. "And if I don't start right this minute, I'll never get done in time."

Although for very different reasons, Theresa's two guidance systems finally have the same idea about what Theresa should do. Her Intelligence-Based Guidance System has been whispering all along, "It would be a good idea to get your taxes done." Now, at the last minute, her Primitive Guidance System is shouting, "Come on, Theresa, hurry up! Get your taxes done NOW!"

Finally, Theresa's intention to get her taxes done is speaking the only language her PGS understands—the language of squeaks. This is now an "emergency," and emergencies are exactly what the PGS was designed to handle.

So, thanks to the same PGS that prevented Theresa from getting her taxes done *early*, Theresa made it to the mailbox *on time*.

Discovering What It Takes To Follow Through

Of course, there's nothing unique about Theresa's experience. What could be more human than putting things off and then finally getting in gear at the last minute? No wonder we operate this way. The *last* minute is often the *first* minute when the PGS is "in synch" with the Intelligence-Based Guidance System. It's the time when our good intentions finally speak the only language the PGS understands—the language of squeaks. Yes, it's at the last minute that our good intentions finally become the squeaky wheels that get the grease they need.

Could we have stumbled upon a simple formula for following through?

Following through requires both intelligent guidance and power. The Intelligence-Based Guidance System has plenty of intelligent guidance but no power. The Primitive Guidance System has plenty of power but no intelligence. We follow through only when the two systems work together—when the Primitive Guidance System pushes us in the same direction that our intentions tell us to go.

What an intriguing possibility! If only we could figure out how to get the PGS to push in the right direction *on command*— if only we could learn how to *work* the Primitive Guidance System rather than *fight* it—we'd be able to use the PGS's muscle to empower our own good intentions.

Book Clubbed

Donna had purchased more than 75 percent of the monthly main selections offered by a mail-order book club for the past quarter of a century.

Is Donna a voracious reader? Not really. She actually read only nine or ten of the 241 books she bought. Did Donna just bite off more than she could chew? Not really. Believe it or not, Donna never intended to buy that many books in the first place. She bought them by "default"; by failing to stop them from coming.

Donna's follow through fiasco started innocently enough when she accepted the book club's "no risk" membership invitation. She still remembers her reaction to the book club's offer:

> Why wouldn't I join? I know I won't buy very many books. But so what? All I have to do is check the "No selection this month" box and send the reply card back. How could anything be easier? How could I possibly lose?

Book and music clubs, and the many other businesses like them, seek to profit by "siding with the hidden flaw." They know something that we mostly ignore: A good intention is a fragile thing indeed. It can be easily defeated by an inconvenience as minor as having to send back a reply card. So while we keep betting on our good intentions, the book clubs keep betting against them. Judging from the proliferation of companies that use the book club approach to sell us more stuff than we intend to buy, siding with the hidden flaw is good business.

CHAPTER 8

Nobody Smokes in Church: The Power and Influence of Situations

Adversity has the effect of eliciting talents, which in prosperous circumstances would have lain dormant.

—Horace

When Kareem Abdul-Jabbar, the former center of the Los Angeles Lakers basketball team, was a college star at UCLA in the late 1960s, he was unstoppable. He dominated the college game with a variety of offensive and defensive skills, including what was arguably his best weapon, the slam dunk.

But, much to Kareem's dismay, during his junior year the situation changed: The NCAA rules committee banned slam dunks.

Kareem didn't spend much time without a deadly weapon. He developed a new shot, later dubbed the "sky hook." Kareem's hook shot eventually became his trademark in the NBA and helped him become a basketball legend.

What's interesting is how Kareem's hook shot was born.

Kareem actually discovered the hook shot in the fourth grade. He loved the feel of the shot. And he knew it would be a winner because it would be impossible to defend against. For many years, Kareem intended to master the hook shot. But somehow he just never got around to putting in the time necessary to do it.

All that changed when the situation changed. When the ban on slam dunks was announced, Kareem began practicing the hook shot constantly. Soon he began to use it in games. Within a short time, his hook shot was solidly in place. Kareem had added a powerful new weapon to his already formidable arsenal.

The story of Kareem's hook shot illustrates a critical but easily overlooked fact of motivational life.

It's the immediate situation—*the full-color, right-in-your-face, what's-happening-right-now-right-this-minute stuff*—that determines whether your PGS will be the friend or the foe of your good intentions. The situation is the key to harnessing the power of the PGS. It's the key to giving your intentions the muscle they need to run the show.

All it took was a change in the situation to get Kareem's PGS to stop working *against* his intention and to start working for it.

The ban on slam dunks stirred Kareem's emotions. He got mad. He believed that the authorities had issued the ban just to undermine his dominance in the game. But Kareem wasn't just angry. His security had been shaken. He had an urgent problem to solve: He had to replace all those points he'd been scoring with the slam dunk. Suddenly the same intention that had been passive for years came to life. It began to squeak loudly. And the PGS—vigilant, reactive, and present-oriented —heard the squeak and came running. This was now an emergency—just the sort of problem the PGS was designed to handle.

Before the situation changed, mastering the hook had been just a "good idea." Now it was a necessity! It *had* to happen. Kareem could finally feel it in his gut instead of just think it in his head. Whenever his intelligent guidance wisely advised, "Master the hook shot," (because it's a great idea), his PGS shouted, "Come on! Hurry Up! Master the hook shot!" (because if you don't, you'll be finished!).

Thanks to the new situation, Kareem's PGS had become his hook shot's best friend. With the PGS finally pushing his intention forward rather than holding it back, Kareem worked on the hook shot with a vengeance. The results were nothing short of spectacular!

Of course, Kareem Abdul-Jabbar didn't deliberately set out to make his intention squeak. It just happened. It was the situation, not Kareem, that turned a powerless intention into an intention "with an attitude." It was the situation that finally got the power of the PGS to push in the same direction that Kareem's intelligent guidance had been telling him to go for years.

How Mia Turned a Sleeper Into a Squeaker

Athletes aren't the only people whose good intentions can get a boost from situations.

Even as a baby, Coby was a night person. Much to his parents' dismay, Coby typically got revved up around

10 P.M. and wanted to play for hours. Nothing his parents did could change this.

As Coby grew older, his tendency to stay up late caused him to have trouble getting up in time for school. There were many frantic scenes in the morning and many missed school busses over the years. It's not that Coby didn't care. He truly hated being late for school. He intended to get up on time. But he just couldn't seem to do it. "I must not be genetically encoded to get up early," he told his mom when he got older. And she was inclined to agree.

The pattern of frantic mornings and missed school busses continued.

Until Coby's sophomore year in high school, that is. That's when the situation changed.

Suddenly, as if by a miracle, Coby awoke with the first ring of the alarm instead of the sixth. He needed no prodding, no yelling, no reminding. He cleaned up, cheerfully got dressed, had breakfast, and was out the door fifteen minutes before the school bus was due.

"What happened to Coby's genetically encoded habit of sleeping till noon?" his father wondered out loud one morning after Coby had dashed out early to wait for the bus.

"Oh, hasn't he told you?" asked Coby's mom.

"Told me what?" he asked.

"About Mia," she replied. "They meet every morning at the bus stop. He's crazy about her."

Before the situation changed—before Coby met Mia—his intention to get up early was a sleeper. It was a smart idea, but it had no muscle. While his intelligent guidance whispered, "Get up" (because being on time will make your life easier), Coby's PGS countered, "Stay in bed" (because it's warm and comfortable). And as long as his PGS worked at cross-purposes with his intelligent guidance, getting out of bed felt like climbing Mount Everest.

After the situation changed—after Coby met Mia—getting up early was a snap! Within seconds of hearing the alarm, Coby would jump out of bed ready for the day.

So, what exactly happened to change Coby? Did he do something to boost his willpower or to develop greater self-discipline? Not at all. All that happened was that the situation changed. Mia entered the picture. And once she did, for Coby, the chance to see Mia squeaked louder than the urge to stay in a warm and cozy bed.

So now when the alarm goes off and Coby's intelligent guidance whispers, "Get up" (because it's the smart thing to do), his PGS roars, "GET UP!" (because I just can't wait to see Mia). And now, with the power of Coby's Primitive Guidance System pushing him to do exactly what his intention has been telling him to do all along, Coby is finally doing it. Thanks to Mia—thanks to the situation—Coby's intention finally has the muscle it needs to get the job done.

Saved By the Bell

It's easy to underestimate the power and influence of situations. Situations, however, can play an absolutely vital role in how our intentions fare. Just ask Joe. He had the biggest possible reason for following through: His life depended on it. Yet the big reason had less impact on his behavior than the situation did.

After his heart attack, Joe was supposed to follow a walking regimen. He did fine at first. But after a few weeks, he got sloppy. When it was time for Joe to walk at the end of the day, he was often too busy, too tired, too hungry, or too something else.

Three months after his heart attack, Joe confessed to his doctor that he was exercising only about half as much as he was supposed to. His doctor gave him a stern warning. He looked Joe straight in the eye and said, "Joe, if you don't do this, you're inviting another heart attack. And the next one could be a lot worse than the last one. For you, walking four times a week could truly be a matter of life and death."

The warning had an immediate impact on Joe. He did really well for the next couple of weeks, but then he started skipping his walks again. This time he got really disgusted with himself. "My God!" he thought, "I must be nuts! My life depends on it, and still I'm not walking regularly. What's especially maddening is that when I do walk, I don't mind it at all."

Joe wasn't nuts. It's just that he expected something to make sense that doesn't make sense. He assumed that because following through was important—it was, after all, a matter of life and death—his intention to walk would always be the squeakiest wheel; that it would easily overpower the far less important desires to have a snack, watch TV, or do something else.

But Joe's PGS didn't give a hoot about how important it was for him to follow through on his intention. To the PGS, all that mattered was squeak.

When it was time for Joe to walk at the end of a long day, what squeaked the most were his hunger, fatigue, and anxiety about the leftover work he brought home with him. The PGS, always busy listening for squeaks, heard them, and came running with the grease. As a result, Joe's intention to walk often took a hike!

Fortunately, things turned out okay for Joe, thanks to the power and influence of situations.

One day, after Joe realized that he had been skipping many more walks than he was taking, the phone rang. It was Tom, a man Joe met during his rehabilitation program. Tom, who had suffered a much more serious heart attack than Joe, was also having trouble following his walking regimen. Tom proposed that the two men walk together. Joe agreed. He liked Tom a lot and was eager to be of help.

Once the situation changed, Joe had no problem following through. From the moment he accepted Tom's proposal, Joe's intention to walk began to squeak loudly enough to get the PGS's grease. Whenever it was time to go walking, Joe's intention would whisper, "Walk" (because it's essential to your health), and his Primitive Guidance System would shout, "WALK!" (because I can't let Tom down).

So with the Primitive Guidance System finally pushing Joe in the same direction that his Intelligence-Based Guidance System had been telling him to go for months, Joe kept on walking.

Joe not only got healthy, he learned an important lesson. Forget about logic. What squeaks, squeaks, and what doesn't, doesn't. Fear of letting Tom down made Joe walk. Wanting to decrease his own chances of having another heart attack didn't. It doesn't matter that it doesn't make sense. The important thing is that it was a change in the situation that finally put Joe's intention in the driver's seat.

A Matter of Luck?

We saw the same scenario played out in the lives of many of the people we interviewed: the situation changes, and suddenly a languishing intention starts to squeak. Then, and only then, the Primitive Guidance System gets behind the intention and starts to push, and presto! Instant follow through!

What intrigued us most was that, with few exceptions, people did nothing to get the ball rolling. They didn't deliberately change the situation to give their intentions the clout they deserved. The situation just changed on its own.

Kareem Abdul-Jabbar didn't wake up one morning and say, "It's about time I made good on my intention to master the hook shot. I think I'll just call the NCAA and ask them to ban the slam dunk. That'll tick me off enough to get me in gear."

Coby never mapped out a strategy to become a morning person by finding an irresistible girlfriend whom he'd have to get up at the crack of dawn to see. Mia just happened to come along.

And Joe, the heart attack victim, was literally "saved by the bell" when his friend telephoned to suggest that they start doing their walking together.

Could following through just be a matter of luck?

Taking the Bull by the Horns

Following through, we discovered, certainly doesn't have to be a matter of luck. We found people out there who deliberately use the powerful effects of situations to follow through. Instead of just waiting for the situation to change, they take the bull by the horns. They "make their own luck" by deliberately changing the situation.

Take Alice, a home-based commodities trader who had lots of "good" reasons to keep her office neat. As good as her reasons were, they just didn't do the trick. "I really should clean up this mess," she would say to herself often.

But then she would usually go and do something else instead. The mess just got deeper and deeper.

About a year ago, all that changed. Alice discovered how to make her intention squeak. Now, once a month— like clockwork—she gets up extra early, rushes to her office, and cleans like mad for an hour. You should see her go!

How did she do it? Simple. She stopped relying on all those "good" reasons for cleaning her office. They made sense. They were important. But they just didn't work. Instead, she deliberately *arranged her environment* to get her intention to squeak.

How? Alice scheduled a 7:00 A.M. meeting in her office once a month with Ron, a highly organized business associate whom Alice admires and wants to impress. "As much as I hate to admit it," Alice explained, "I'm far more motivated to impress Ron than I am to have a neat office. I realized that I would absolutely die of embarrassment if he ever saw the mess in my office." And that's exactly why she invited him there!

So, at 6:00 A.M. on the first Tuesday of every month, you'll find Alice—her Primitive Guidance System working like a powerful bulldozer to push her hard to avoid embarrassment—cleaning her office. And thanks to the situation she *created*, Alice finally has the neat office she's always wanted.

And then there's Nick, who not only took the bull by the horns, he threw the bull over his head.

Nick, a real estate investor, had spent the better part of three decades struggling to lose some of his 360 pounds. Fed up with traditional weight-loss programs, Nick decided that the time had come to get out the heavy artillery. He identified the enemy—eating like a pig in restaurants—and declared all-out war.

Nick thought things through. He decided that he should stay out of restaurants altogether. He knew, though, that unless he could find a way to make his intention squeak loudly enough, his powerful appetite for restaurant food would (pardon the pun) have his good intention for lunch. So he created just the right kind of situation—he *arranged his environment*—to give his intention more clout.

How? Nick put his money and his reputation on the line. He had "Wanted" posters printed up and placed in all his favorite restaurants. Each poster featured a photo of Nick, looking his hungriest, and offered a $25,000 reward to anyone who spotted him eating in a restaurant.

The result: Whenever Nick would approach a restaurant, instead of shouting, "Yum, yum, let's eat!" his PGS would shout, "Stay away! You'll lose your money and your reputation."

Nick lost 114 pounds.

Like Alice, Nick didn't just rely on his good intentions to get the job done. To the contrary, he took rather extreme measures to follow through. Although he may have gone further than most people would dare go, his story illustrates what it really takes to follow through:

The key to getting the power of the PGS to push you in the same direction that your intentions tell you to go is to deliberately *arrange your environment*—deliberately create situations—to make your good intentions squeak.

As Nick and Alice realized, having an intention is not enough. It's only the first step in a two-step process. In the next chapter, we'll show you how one man, frustrated by his failure to follow through, discovered how to take the second step. And thanks to *Step Two,* he was able to solve a problem that had been eating away at him for years.

CHAPTER 9

Discovering Step Two

The people who get on in this world are the people who get up and look for the circumstances they want, and, if they can't find them, make them.

—George Bernard Shaw

Wayne's roofing business was in trouble. He had just lost another big job that the business really needed in order to make ends meet. Wayne knew that it wasn't just a matter of bad luck. He had done it to himself. And it was hardly the first time.

Wayne was losing business as a result of his bad habit of being late in sending out quotations to prospective customers. Of all the tasks he had to perform to keep his business going, preparing quotations was his least favorite. "I hate it," he would often tell his wife. "I just hate it."

Wayne usually showed up promptly to check out prospective jobs. But then he would typically put off preparing quotations for weeks. Many customers got tired of waiting. They went ahead and did business with other roofing contractors. And as the word got around that it might take Wayne forever to submit a quotation, prospective new customers thought twice before contacting Wayne's company in the first place.

Wayne knew he had a problem and he took it seriously. He would often stop to give himself a good scolding. "I've got to start getting those quotes out right away," he would tell himself. "This is ruining my business."

After every scolding, things would get better for a while. But before he knew it, Wayne would be back to his old habit of putting off quotations.

Hands-Off and Going Nowhere

It was obvious that Wayne had been taking a hands-off approach to his good intention. Although he had decided what he should do to run his business more effectively, when it came to implementing his decision, he did nothing but cross his fingers and hope for the best.

Without realizing it, Wayne subscribed to the *It Must Be Me* theory. He assumed that because his intention to get quotes out quickly was so important to him, he'd follow through; that if he didn't, it would be his own fault. Thinking this way is what prevented Wayne from solving the problem.

Discovering Step Two

I (Pete) decided to introduce Wayne to a new way of thinking about his intention—one that would give him a really good shot at following through.

"Wayne," I asked, "do you ever need to get up early?"

"Every single workday," he replied. "I have to wake up at 5:30 in the morning."

"So, I suppose you just automatically wake up on your own at 5:30 every morning. Is that right?" I asked.

"Yeah right," Wayne chuckled. "On my own, I'd probably sleep until at least 8 or 9, maybe even later. On the weekends sometimes I sleep until 10 or 11," he confessed.

"So how do you manage to wake up at 5:30?" I asked.

"I set my alarm clock," he replied.

"I see," I said. "But why would you need an alarm clock to wake you up at 5:30, if you've decided to wake up at 5:30?" I asked.

"Well, without the alarm clock, I'd just keep on sleeping," replied Wayne. He looked puzzled.

"How do you know?" I asked.

"I've tried it. I mean, once in a while, I forget to set the alarm. I definitely don't wake up on my own," he explained.

"Even though you've decided?" I asked.

"Yeah. Deciding sure as heck doesn't wake me up," he chuckled.

"Wayne, let me make sure I understand. You make the decision to wake up early. But you don't just stop there. That's because you already know from experience that deciding isn't enough; that you won't wake up on your own. So instead of just crossing your fingers and hoping for the best, you take another step. You set your alarm clock. You make sure that something will happen to wake you up. Does that sound right?" I asked.

"Well, I never thought of it that way," said Wayne. "I just do it. But yeah, I guess that's right."

"So, following through on your intention to get up at 5:30 A.M. is a two-step process, isn't it? Step One is deciding what to do. And Step Two is arranging your environment—'setting the alarm clock'—to make sure that something will push you to actually do what you've decided to do. Does that make sense to you?" I asked.

"Yeah it does," he said.

"Good. Then let's talk about your decision to send out

quotations on time, okay? Are you doing what you've decided to do?" I asked.

"No, I'm definitely not," replied Wayne.

"So it's just like waking up early, isn't it? You already know from experience that just taking Step One—just deciding to get the quotations out on time—is not enough to get you to actually do it. Is that right?" I asked.

"I think I see what you're getting at. I have to 'set the alarm clock,' don't I? I have to get something to push me to do what I've decided to do. I guess I have to take Step Two, don't I?" asked Wayne with a twinkle in his eye.

"You've got it," I said. "So let's talk about how to take Step Two."

"Okay. How do I do it?" Wayne asked. "I mean, waking up early is one thing. I just set the alarm. But what can I do to make sure that something will push me to get those damned quotes out on time?"

"Now you're asking the right question! Let's see if we can put our heads together and come up with an answer," I replied.

Setting the Alarm Clock

Once Wayne understood what Step Two was all about, he didn't have much trouble figuring out how to "set the alarm clock" to make sure he would follow through on his "get those quotes out on time" intention. He came up with a great plan, and he implemented it. When we spoke with him three months later, Wayne told us that since taking Step Two, he had gotten every single quotation out on time. His business—and his confidence—had improved dramatically.

What exactly did Wayne do to turn things around? What was his Step Two? Well, all it took to change his situation was a five-minute conversation with Bev, his assistant. It wasn't just any conversation, though.

Wayne told Bev that he would give her a ten-dollar bonus for each and every quotation that went out within forty-eight hours of his on-site visit. (As he conducted as many as ten on-site visits a week, the bonuses could really add up.) Wayne then invited Bev to put together a new system for keeping track of the quotations due, and he urged her to remind him—to pester him if necessary—to get the quotations done on time.

Wayne knew that by offering Bev bonuses for getting the quotations out on time, she would be motivated to push him to get the job done. More importantly, he knew that he was a softhearted fellow—the sort of person who couldn't bear the thought of depriving Bev of the ten-dollar bonuses he promised her. If she pushed, he figured, he would respond. He was right.

Wayne was a little surprised at first to discover just how motivated he was by his desire to avoid standing between Bev and her bonuses—in fact, much more motivated than he was by his genuine desire to be successful in business. Although this caused him to shake his head once in a while, Wayne was not about to argue with success. "Setting the alarm clock" to make sure that he would follow through on his intention was definitely working.

Wayne is now a great believer in the importance of taking Step Two. It's no wonder. Thanks to Step Two, he now runs his business—and his life—more effectively. He no longer tries to follow through by keeping his fingers crossed. He takes the bull by the horns. When he decides to do something, he doesn't just stop there. He "sets the alarm clock." He deliberately arranges his environment to make sure that his good intentions will squeak loudly enough to get the grease they need to get the job done.

As Wayne himself now puts it, "Leaving out Step Two is like deciding to wake up early without setting your alarm clock."

CHAPTER 10

The Art of Shaping Situations

We shape our houses, and afterwards our houses shape us.
—Winston Churchill

Winston Churchill understood the importance of deliberately designing situations to help people behave in accord with their intentions. When it came time to rebuild the House of Commons, which had been destroyed in an air raid, Churchill vigorously opposed the notion that every member of the House should have "a desk to sit at and a lid to bang." He argued that the new House should have fewer seats than members. That way members would feel a sense of "crowd and urgency" that would encourage them to conduct themselves like the active lawmakers they promised to be. In urging members to carefully consider the powerful effect that their new environment would have on their behavior, Churchill said, "We shape our houses, and afterwards our houses shape us."

The key to taking Step Two is to "shape your house"—to

deliberately change the situation or the way you experience it—so that it will help you do what you intend to do.

But how exactly do you go about the business of shaping situations? Setting your alarm clock so that you wake up on time is one thing. But what can you do to make sure that you'll follow through on your intention to, say, be less critical of your spouse or keep your checkbook balanced?

In this chapter, we'll show you how Mark, Brian, and Sheila took Step Two; how they shaped their situations to make their intentions effective.

Asking the Right Question

Mark, Brian, and Sheila each had different intentions and different reasons for failing to follow through. But they all began Step Two the same way: They *diagnosed* before they *treated.*

They each began by asking this question:

How can I shape the situation, or the way I experience it, to make my intention the squeakiest wheel?

Mark vs. Anger

Mark was doing a lousy job of following through on his intention to refrain from yelling at his teenage son, Jeff. Whenever Jeff would come home late, defiantly neglect his homework or chores, or talk back to Mark and his wife, Mark would become absolutely furious. Despite his conviction that yelling would only make matters worse, Mark ended up yelling almost every time.

Mark began by asking himself, "What's the problem here? What's keeping me from following through on this intention?" The answer was obvious: Every time Jeff acted irresponsibly, while Mark's intention would barely whisper, "Keep your cool. Yelling will only make things worse," Mark's PGS would shout, "Attack! Don't let that kid get away with this!"

It was no wonder Mark wasn't following through. His PGS—with all its power—was urging him to do exactly the opposite of what his intention was telling him to do.

Mark knew he had to make his intention the squeakiest wheel. "I need to do something," Mark reasoned, "to change the way I experience my confrontations with Jeff. I need to find a way to *feel* like keeping my mouth shut." In other words, Mark needed to get his PGS involved. If he could get his PGS to shout, "Don't yell," instead of just "Let him have it," Mark would follow through.

An idea came to Mark with a smile. "I'll make a promise to Jeff. I'll tell him that I'll extend his curfew if I yell at him."

No, Mark hadn't lost his marbles. To the contrary, he discovered some very useful new marbles. He discovered how to shape the situation to make himself *feel* like doing the right thing.

The last thing Mark wanted to do when Jeff behaved irresponsibly was to reward him with more freedom. Therefore, by making his promise to Jeff, Mark could create a here-and-now threat that would grab the PGS's attention. So instead of continuing to experience Jeff's irresponsible behavior with an overpowering, "Let him have it!" he would now feel an insistent "My God, if I yell, I'll have to give that irresponsible kid even more freedom."

The follow through strategy worked like a charm. Mark's intention was finally speaking the PGS's language. Instead of just urging him to yell, Mark's PGS started urging him to refrain from yelling.

By deliberately changing the situation, Mark was able to

get the power of the PGS to push him to do exactly what his intention had been telling him to do all along.

Brian vs. Candy

Brian had a different kind of battle to fight. Getting too mad wasn't his problem; getting too hungry was. Even though he decided to stick to a low-calorie diet, Brian just loved the yummy candy bars in the vending machine right outside his office. He joked about the "magnetic field" that pulled him to the candy machine against his will. But Brian wasn't laughing about what the candy was doing to his weight.

As Brian would walk to the machine with his mouth watering, he would tell himself for the thousandth time, "Brian, this isn't good for you. You're going to gain weight. Keep this up, and you'll look like your father. You'll have the physique of a walrus." But Brian's PGS wasn't in the least bit interested in the future. It was only interested in *right now*. It would scream, "Oh boy! Reese's Peanut Butter Cups! Now!"

Despite his good intention, some days Brian had as many as three candy bars. Each time he gave in to his craving, he felt guilty and frustrated. "I can't believe how little willpower I have," he would say to himself. He scolded himself over and over again. But nothing changed. He was well on his way to "Walrusdom" when Brian discovered Step Two.

Brian knew what the problem was. His craving for candy was simply overpowering his intention. "I've got to turn things around. I've got to get my 'no candy bar' intention to *outsqueak* my craving," he thought.

Brian came up with three options:

1. He could do something to make his "no candy bar" intention *feel* more important—to make it squeak louder.

2. He could do something that would turn down the volume on his craving.
3. He could do both.

Right off the bat, Brian thought of two strategies he could use to make his "no candy bar" intention a much squeakier wheel.

First, he could add some horsepower to his intention. Instead of just relying on his concerns about his weight, he could give himself another reason to follow through. Brian knew how important it was to him to be seen by others as a man of his word. So he decided to announce to his coworkers that he was *definitely* not going to have any more candy bars. By putting his reputation on the line this way, he created another reason— one that was much more compelling and *right now*—for following through on his "no candy bar" intention.

Second, Brian figured he could make his intention squeak a lot louder if he could find a way to make the long-term consequences of eating too much candy *feel* real *right now*. That was easy. He would keep a photo of his grossly overweight father on his desk right near the phone so that he'd see it every time the phone would ring. And he'd label the photo, "Brian Beware."

Brian was just beginning to devise a strategy for reducing his craving for candy when a memo came across his desk. The memo asked for volunteers to move to newly remodeled office space one floor down and all the way at the other end of the building—a good two- to three-minute hike from the nearest candy machine. "Hmm," Brian thought to himself. "This is perfect! By moving, I can kill two birds with one stone. If I'm that far away from the candy machine, I bet I won't feel the craving as often. And even when I do, the extra time and effort required to get the candy bar will help discourage me from doing it."

By implementing the strategies he came up with, Brian managed to change how he experienced the whole candy bar situation. Because he wasn't walking by the tempting vending machine anymore, he didn't crave candy as often. And whenever he did, instead of just shouting, "Eat that candy," his PGS had a lot more to say. It also shouted, "Don't do it! Jay and Pam and Phyllis will think you're a weak-willed wimp!" And it also shouted, "Don't do it! You'll end up fat like your dad!" And it also shouted, "Don't do it! Who wants to walk all the way up there and back?"

With his intention now getting help from his coworkers, his dad, and the long walk, Brian's "incurable" candy bar problem got dramatically better.

Sheila vs. Paperwork

The pile of undone paperwork on Sheila's desk was really beginning to bug her. She knew that sooner or later she'd be in deep trouble if she didn't get caught up. She knew she had to do something. But what?

Once Sheila discovered Step Two, she stopped spinning her wheels and started asking the right questions. "What's keeping me from following through?" she asked. The answer was obvious: She absolutely hated doing paperwork. "The very thought of spending hours working on my paperwork just makes me sick," she exclaimed.

The problem was that Sheila's intense dislike of paperwork had such a firm grip on her PGS that her "Do paperwork" intention didn't have a prayer. Her PGS was driving her as far away as possible from the stack of papers on her desk.

To solve the problem, Sheila first considered doing something to turn up the heat, that is, doing something that would make her feel compelled to do the paperwork even though she hated it. She thought about sending a memo to her not-so-forgiving boss confessing her paperwork sins and promising to get caught up by the end of the month. Sheila knew her boss and knew herself. She knew that changing the situation this way would do the trick. It would eliminate the wiggle room that allowed her to keep putting off the paperwork. It would put enough pressure on her to get the job done.

But she hesitated. Something didn't feel quite right.

"I know this plan will work, and I'll certainly use it if I have to," she thought. "But it makes me a little nervous. And besides, how is this going to help me in the long run? I sure don't want to be sending memos like this to my boss every month."

So Sheila decided to go down a different path. She wondered if instead of trying to make her intention squeak louder, she could quiet down her distaste for paperwork. "Is there anything I can do to make my paperwork feel less burdensome so that I won't feel so compelled to avoid it?" she asked herself.

The question led Sheila to an interesting insight. "No wonder I avoid paperwork like the plague. I make it much worse than it has to be by expecting myself to sit down and work on it for hours at a stretch."

Sheila felt like she was on to something. "If I knew I could spend no more than, say, a half hour at a time doing paperwork, I think it would make a big difference. I still wouldn't like it. But if I had to face only a *hill* of unpleasant work, instead of what feels like a huge mountain, I think I could do it."

Sheila liked the idea of turning down the heat better than turning it up. But she wasn't quite convinced that the gentler approach would work. Still, she decided, it was worth a try. "I have nothing to lose," she figured. "If it doesn't work, I can always send the memo."

So here's how Sheila took Step Two:

She entered three thirty-minute "Do paperwork" appointments in her calendar every week for the rest of the month.

Just to make sure that she'd always experience these paperwork appointments as *hills* rather than *mountains,* Sheila made a point of scheduling something else immediately after each of the paperwork appointments. That way the worst that could happen is that she'd have a very unpleasant half hour.

Before closing her calendar, Sheila made one more entry. On the page for the last day of the month, she wrote:

"Is it time for THE MEMO?"

Sheila wanted to remind herself that if the kinder, gentler approach didn't work, she'd have to roll out the heavy artillery.

Fortunately, the "turn down the heat" strategy worked. It loosened the grip Sheila's intense dislike of paperwork had on the PGS. And with the PGS no longer pushing her hard to avoid the paperwork, her intention was finally able to get the job done.

Using the Right Tools

Instead of just crossing their fingers and hoping for the best, Mark, Brian, and Sheila took the bull by the horns. They took Step Two.

But they each used different follow through strategies— different tools—to get the job done. They each chose strategies that zeroed in on their own particular reasons for not following through.

Sheila changed the situation so that what she *felt like doing* no longer interfered with what she *intended to do.* In other words, she got her PGS to stop working so fervently against her intention. Mark and Brian changed the situation so that what they *intended to do* and what they *felt like doing* became one and the same. In other words, they got the PGS to work *for* their good intentions instead of against them.

Using the right tools for the job is always important. You wouldn't use a sledgehammer to tighten a tiny screw on your eyeglasses. Neither would you use a tiny screwdriver to break up an old cement patio. When it comes to taking Step Two, using the *right* tools means using the follow through strategies that give your intentions precisely the help they need.

In the chapters that follow, we'll introduce you to the most effective follow through strategies we've discovered. We'll help you create a personal follow through toolkit that contains the basic strategies you need to tackle virtually any follow through problem you face.

Is All This Really Necessary?

Still a little skeptical? Is there a little voice in your head that's wondering, "Is all this really necessary? Do I really have to make such a big deal about following through?"

Well, the answer is, "Only if you want to follow through!"

If you're not yet convinced that the "Cross your fingers" approach to follow through doesn't work; if you still believe that having a good intention is all it takes to follow through, then, please, stop right here. Close this book and set it aside for a while.

Then, as you once again go about the business of living, try to notice what happens to your good intentions. If you do, you'll be back. And you'll be ready to give Step Two a try.

More and More Grist for the Intention Mill

"And in the economic news today, we have this report:

'The annual production of good intentions is rising. So is the price of poor follow through.' "

In this fast-paced, information-rich, high-tech world, success increasingly depends on being able to actually do what we intend to do.

With more information available every day about what we can do, for example, to stay healthy or get wealthy, to raise happy drug-free kids, or to protect the environment, we know more all the time about how to get what we want out of life. With so much grist for the intention mill, it's no wonder we produce so many intentions.

The more we know, the more potential we have for improving our lives. But useful new information doesn't automatically change what we do. The only way we humans can actually benefit from much of the useful information we keep accumulating is by adopting intentions and following through on them. So, the more we know about what we could do to make our lives better, the more potential we're wasting by doing a lousy job of following through.

For example, if researchers discovered that eating at an unnaturally slow pace could add ten years or more to your life, you wouldn't *automatically* start eating slowly. You'd have to decide to do that. What's more, you'd have to *keep on* deciding. Your ability to actually benefit from the potentially life-extending new information would hinge entirely on your ability to follow through.

It's ironic that the more technological, social, and economic progress we humans make, the more demands we place on our decidedly unimpressive follow through equipment.

For example, because advances in technology have made life so much less physically demanding than it once was, we now have to *decide* to get regular exercise in order to stay healthy. The problem is, a group of one hundred people *today* who only *intend* to get enough exercise will probably produce less exercise than did a group of ten people *yesterday* who *had* to be physically active just to survive.

And what about the affluence we enjoy? Just think about the burden that "having plenty" places on our ability to follow through.

For example, many of yesterday's parents criticize today's parents for making life much too easy for their kids. "Stop giving your children everything they want!" insist the parents of yesterday. "Don't you see that you're depriving your children of the character-building effects of having to work hard and be patient? You have to say 'No.' "

What the critics of today's parents don't take into account is that it was a whole lot easier to say No to kids in less affluent times. It's one thing to say No when, economically, you're in no position to say Yes. It's something else entirely to *decide* to say No when you know darned well that you have the means to make your child happy right now by saying Yes. In today's more affluent times, when saying No stems from a philosophical decision rather than an economic necessity, "building character" in our children depends far more than it used to on the ability of parents to follow through on their intentions.

We humans keep putting more and more of our eggs in our follow through basket. And until we plug the hole in the basket, we can look forward to a whole lot more scrambled eggs.

Follow Through Strategies

The game of life is not so much in holding a good hand as playing a poor hand well.

—H. T. Leslie

Follow Through Strategies: An Overview

In this section, we'll introduce you to specific follow through strategies that grew out of our discoveries about how the mind treats good intentions.

Rather than offer you a bunch of "recipes," we're going to teach you how to "cook." We'll rely on examples to show you how to first size up your own intentions and then choose the right strategies to get the job done.

Each strategy represents a useful way to understand and solve follow through problems. Each takes a different approach to making your intentions more effective. For example, we'll teach you one strategy that helps you follow through by stimulating your desire to do what you intend to do. We'll teach you another strategy that works by making it difficult or even impossible for you to do the "wrong" thing.

What's important to understand is that each follow through technique is a useful, practical tool—not an entire toolkit. The more tools you learn how to use, the better equipped you'll be to follow through on any intention you decide to adopt.

We'll begin by introducing you to the two master strategies we call *Spotlighting* and *Willpower Leveraging*. We refer to these as master strategies because they address what we believe are the two most fundamental causes of poor follow through. Spotlighting keeps your good intentions from getting lost in the shuffle. Willpower Leveraging helps you get the biggest "bang" out of each "buck" of willpower you spend.

Also in this section is the story of a remarkable little device, called the MotivAider®, that allows you to make sure your good intentions will get all the attention they need to be effective.

CHAPTER 11

Master Strategy #1: Spotlighting

In *Leaves of Grass*, poet Walt Whitman wrote,

> *Do I contradict myself?*
> *Very well then, I contradict myself.*
> *I am large, I contain multitudes.*

We all contain "multitudes." The mind plays host to a myriad of inner "voices." In the crowd at any given moment are countless needs, wants, fears, values, beliefs, and good intentions. Each voice has its own idea of what we should do. Each voice has its own distinct point of view.

Just ask Julia. She recently decided to become a real estate agent. She's wanted to do it for years. But she finally took the plunge. Julia signed up to take her licensing exam in three months. She dipped into the family's meager savings to pay for the registration fee and buy an expensive home study course. She's committed. Now it's time to get down to business and start studying. And that's precisely what Julia intends to do.

Let's interview just a few of the voices in Julia's mind to see where they stand relative to Julia's intention.

"Excuse me, you in the front row. What's your position on studying for the real estate exam?"

"I'm in favor of studying because I want to pass the exam so I can get my license and earn a better income so that my family can afford the things we really want."

"How about you over there? Where do you stand?"

"I'm in favor of studying because passing a hard test will be a boost to my self-confidence."

"How about you over there on the right?"

"I'm in favor of studying because I believe in finishing what I start. I've signed up for the test, now I've got to study for it."

"How about you?"

"I'm all for it. I can't stand my boss. She's an absolute witch. If I pass the test I can say goodbye to her once and for all."

"How about you in the second row? Where do you stand?"

"I'm in favor because I'd be terribly embarrassed if I failed the test. People would think I was not very smart. I'd hate that."

"How about you? What's your position?"

"No way! I hate studying. It's sooo boring."

"And how about you over there on the left?"

"I'm against it. Studying stresses me out."

"How about you?"

"Me? I'm against it. The kids don't get enough of my time as it is. If I study, I'll be neglecting them."

"And you over there in the back? What's your position on studying?"

"Studying? Sorry, but after a long day at work, I'd much rather watch TV. I deserve to relax."

There are indeed many voices in Julia's crowd that have an opinion about whether or not she should study for the exam. Some enthusiastically support her intention. Some just as enthusiastically oppose it. If Julia listens to the voices that favor studying, she'll burn the midnight oil. If she listens to the voices that oppose studying, she'll burn no oil at all. If she listens to both—you guessed it—she'll have a struggle on her hands.

Because the voices she listens to the most will have the biggest say in how she behaves, it makes a big difference which voices get Julia's attention. In fact, it could make the difference between following through and fizzling out.

So, of the many voices in Julia's mind that take a stand on whether or not she should study, which ones will actually get her attention?

If you think it's entirely up to Julia, you're wrong. It seems like she *should* be in full control of which voices she tunes in to. But she isn't—no more than *you're* in control of which voices in *your* crowd get *your* attention.

Harnessing the Power of Cues

In this chapter, we'll introduce you to Spotlighting, a strategy that helps you follow through by putting you in charge of which voices you listen to.

The beauty of Spotlighting is that it allows you to turn a liability into an asset. It enables you to benefit from the mind's often troublesome tendency to let the things around you— rather than your own intelligent guidance—determine which voices you'll listen to and, therefore, how you'll behave.

Spotlighting is an "If you can't beat 'em, join 'em" way to solve the problem of having a mind that won't automatically stay focused on good intentions. In Spotlighting, instead of trying to make yourself less distractible—less susceptible to being influenced by what you see, hear, smell, taste, and feel at the moment—you celebrate how distractible you really are. You keep yourself on track by making sure that you're exposed to the *right* distractions—distractions that focus your attention on the right voices.

Spotlighting lets you take advantage of the enormous potential that "cues" have to influence your behavior.

Cues are the things "out there" that cause you to pay attention to particular voices—to particular needs, wants, fears, values, beliefs, and good intentions. A cue is a stimulus, a catalyst, a switch. Cues stimulate, activate, and energize voices.

Cues make the voices speak up so that they have a greater say in how you behave.

It happens every day. The sight of a gruesome picture on the front page of the newspaper energizes your "What happened?" voice. You stop to check out the story even though you were in a big hurry to get home. The smell of fresh cookies wafting through a shopping mall stimulates your "I want something yummy to eat" voice. You stop to get a chocolate chip "fix" even though you were on your way to the sock shop to look for a gift for your niece. The sound of a new clicking noise coming from your engine compartment activates your "I want to keep my car in good condition" voice. You decide to stop and get your car serviced after having put it off for weeks.

A cue works like a spotlight. It focuses your attention on a particular voice in the crowd and makes that voice stand out.

Of course, cues don't create voices. They simply empower the voices that are already there. They do it by "changing the channel." Cues tune you in to particular voices that would otherwise remain lost in the crowd.

It happens, for example, when you see a big, juicy burger on your TV screen and suddenly you feel as though you won't be whole again until you eat one. It happens when you hear about a parent who lost a child and suddenly you feel like spending more time with your own children. It happens when you see someone you know who looks and feels great after losing fifteen pounds, and suddenly you feel like going to the health club again. It happens when you hear a rousing speech at a convention, and suddenly feel like you can make all your dreams come true.

We're continuously exposed to cues. And because the particular cues we happen to be exposed to determine which of our voices we'll listen to and, therefore, which of our voices will have the biggest say in how we behave, it matters a great deal which cues we're exposed to. Yet as much as it matters, we usually just take whatever comes our way. We miss a golden opportunity to give a say to the right voices by deliberately choosing which cues we'll be exposed to.

Spotlighting is using cues *on purpose* to empower the right voices. Spotlighting is a way to keep yourself tuned in to the particular voices in the crowd that make you actually *feel* like doing what your intentions are telling you to do.

To use Spotlighting effectively, you have to first be able to recognize the powerful effect that cues typically have on your own behavior. The more aware you are of how cues normally affect you, the better job you can do of using cues deliberately to help you follow through.

Which Is the Real David?

David is a bright, ambitious young executive who came to see me (Steve) several years ago because he was frustrated by his failure to live up to his full potential at work. David told me about an experience he once had that had opened his eyes to the power of cues.

Thanks to an unexpected phone call, David had gotten a late start to the airport. As he grabbed his briefcase and kissed his wife goodbye, she reminded him, as she always did, to drive safely. David assured her that he would. "Why wouldn't I?" he thought.

But as he headed for the airport, each time David glanced at the clock on his dashboard, he became more anxious. In order for him to make it, everything would have to go perfectly. There was absolutely no time to spare. No slack. No time for traffic. No time for mishaps.

David sped up as he approached a green light so that he would get through the intersection before the light turned red. Then he swerved around a car that had slowed down to turn right. He kept checking his mirrors to look for police. He knew he was speeding, but he was in a big hurry.

Suddenly the traffic slowed and David saw flashing lights up ahead. "Oh no," he thought to himself. "Now I'll never make it." He was really annoyed. But as he got closer, he realized that there had been a serious accident. As he drove slowly past the accident scene, he got a glimpse of a bloody victim being lifted out of one of the twisted cars on the road. He noticed the victim's arms hanging limply. Then David saw a young girl, who looked to be about his daughter's age, crying uncontrollably in the arms of a police officer.

As David drove past the accident scene, he felt himself trembling. He took a deep breath. "That could have been me," he said to himself. "I can't believe how recklessly I was driving. How stupid it is to take a chance on getting killed or killing someone else just to get to the airport on time," he scolded himself.

As David continued on to the airport, he was a different person, or at least a different driver. He paid close attention to traffic and to his speedometer. He checked the mirrors often, only this time he wasn't looking for police, he was checking for other cars. David had suddenly become the very model of safe driving. In a matter of seconds, seeing the accident had transformed him from a reckless driver to a careful driver.

"You know, I've thought a lot about what happened to me that day," David told me. "It kind of bothered me. I kept wondering which was the real me. Was I the reckless driver before the accident, or the careful driver after the accident?" David wondered. "Now that I understand this stuff about cues and voices, it all makes sense to me. I guess I was—and I still am—both drivers, both people. I mean, I have the potential to be either reckless or responsible. It all depends on which voices I'm paying attention to. And often it's not me—it's the stuff going on around me—that gets to pick the voices."

Using Cues on Purpose

David needed no further convincing. He had already experienced the power of cues for himself. He was ready and eager to learn how to use cues on purpose to stimulate the right voices. He was all set to try out Spotlighting.

I asked David to select one of the several intentions that had been getting lost in the shuffle. He didn't hesitate at all.

David explained that he did a good job with the technical aspects of his work. But as a people-manager, he was weak. He just wasn't being a good motivator. It wasn't that he lacked skill, it was that he would typically get so involved with the nuts and bolts of projects that he'd more or less ignore the human element, that is, until it was too late.

"I've gotten lots of feedback from people I respect that I don't do a good job of motivating my people," David explained. "I don't make them feel important and appreciated—like they're valued members of a team. I know it causes problems. The funny thing is, I think they're terrific. I'm always bragging to others about what a great staff I have. I keep promising myself that whenever someone does a good job, I'll be sure to let them know. It's not that I'm at all reluctant to do it. It's just that I get caught up in other things and I forget."

"Okay, David," I said. "Let's see if we can use Spotlighting to help you follow through on your intention to be a better motivator.

"Spotlighting involves three steps. First, you need to identify the right voices—the needs or wants or motives that urge you to do the same thing your intention is telling you to do. Next, you need to identify or create the right cues—the things out there that will stimulate those voices. And third, you need to find a way to make sure that you'll be exposed to enough of the right cues. Are you with me?" I asked.

"So far," David replied.

"Okay," I said. "Let's begin by identifying the right voices. David, can you think of a need or want or fear that would urge you to make your people feel important and appreciated? In other words, is there a voice in there that, if you listened to it, would make you feel like following through on your good intentions?"

"Yes, there is," David answered. "Not that you'd know it from the way I've been treating my staff, but I really do want to make a positive difference in people's lives. I coach Little League baseball and I love it because I have a chance to make kids feel good about themselves."

"Okay, so there is a David in that busy mind of yours that really wants to validate people," I said. "If we could shine a spotlight on that particular David—if we could really make him stand out from the other voices in the crowd—he would urge you to make your people feel good about themselves, right? So let's see if we can figure out a way to keep that particular voice in the spotlight.

"We need to find a switch that will turn on that particular voice. David, tell me about the times when you feel most like making people feel good about themselves—the times when you're most tuned in to that particular desire."

"Well, that's easy," replied David. "It's when I'm coaching Little League baseball. I'll tell you, I see those kids in their uniforms and I know instantly that I'm there to help build confidence and teamwork, not to win games. The neat thing is, my team is actually doing better than most of the teams coached by dads who focus only on winning and who lose the kids in the process. If I could just coach my staff the way I coach my Little League kids, hey, I'd have it made."

"Okay, David," I continued, "so if we could find a way to keep you tuned in at the office to your Little League coaching experience, we'd be able to make the right voice stand out in the crowd, right?

"So let's see if we can find a switch—a cue—to turn on this voice, to put it in the spotlight, to empower it. What could you do at the office to remind yourself of your Little League experience?" I asked.

"I suppose one thing I could do is put a photo of my Little League team on my desk," answered David.

"How about putting it in front of your phone so that you'll see it whenever you answer the phone," I suggested. "What else can you do? The more cues the better."

David thought for a while and then said, "I guess I could bring a baseball cap to my office and hang it on the coatrack near the door. I suppose I could also use the baseball memo pads my kids gave me as a gift last summer. They have baseball symbols and quotes on them. I send lots of brief handwritten notes to my staff. In fact, I could also put some baseball language in the boilerplate paragraphs I include in various routine memos to the staff. I always read these memos thoroughly before they go out, so I'd notice the baseball stuff and it would remind me to make sure I'm coaching, not just telling."

"These are great ideas, David," I said. "Anything at all you can do to stimulate that 'David the coach' voice will help. The more you can surround yourself at the office with things that trigger the way you are when you're coaching, the more successful you'll be."

David began to laugh. "You know, what would really do the trick is if my staff wore baseball uniforms! I'd never forget to coach them. I know that's totally ridiculous, but it would work."

"You bet it would," I said. "Even though you can't actually do that, it shows that you're barking up the right tree. You know what you're aiming for. The more you can surround yourself with right-in-your-face cues that make it impossible for you to forget that you're there to coach, the better job you'll do of following through on your intention.

"Now David, if you implement these ideas and you still don't follow through, it's probably because you're being exposed to too many of the wrong cues—cues that are keeping you tuned in to the wrong voice. I'm referring to the 'Hurry up and get it done right, right now' voice. When you listen only to that voice, you obviously forget about your intention to be a good coach. We'll have to see if we can identify the cues that tune you in to the wrong voice and then find a way to reduce your exposure to them."

"You mean like when I look at my project management computer program a dozen times a day and see how little time I have to get a big job done?" David wondered. "Or when I hang out with Jack, who's always talking about work as if it were a race?"

"Exactly," I replied. "You see, the more you're exposed to the wrong cues, the more tuned in you'll be to the wrong voice. And the more you're exposed to the right cues, the more tuned in you'll be to the right voice. The key, then, is to surround yourself with as many of the right cues and as few of the wrong cues as possible. For now, let's just see if adding enough of the right cues will do the trick."

David got excellent results. Surrounding himself with the right cues kept him tuned in to the right voice. He was finally following through on his intention to be a good coach to his staff.

David Gets "MotivAided"[1]

Pleased with his success, David was eager to tackle another problem that had plagued him for years. "My posture stinks," David told me. "I'm concerned about it because I think it can give people the wrong impression of me. One of my coworkers keeps telling me that my slouching makes me look really bored at meetings. That's sure not going to help my career."

David explained that he'd tried dozens of times to improve his posture. "Each time I try, the same thing happens. At first, I remember to straighten up. But after a while, I start forgetting. Soon, I'm forgetting more than I'm remembering. And before long, I'm slouching all the time again. It's really frustrating. It should be such a simple problem to solve. I really don't want to slouch, and I have no reason to avoid straightening my back. In fact, it feels good when I do it. Would Spotlighting help me solve this problem?"

"David, your intention to improve your posture is exactly the kind of intention that begs for Spotlighting. The one and only reason you don't keep your back straight is that you don't remember. And the reason you don't remember is that your mind is busy, your life is busy, and there aren't enough cues out there to remind you. You have no reluctance whatsoever to straighten your back. There's no resistance, no reason to avoid doing it, no competing voices, no tug of war. All it would take to improve your posture is being able to keep your intention in the spotlight—to keep it on the front burner."

"Yeah," said David, "it's sure not there now."

"David," I asked, "are there times when you do remember to straighten your back?"

David thought for a few minutes. "Yeah. I did when I noticed my friend Judd slouching. And once when I noticed that I was getting close to the edge of my seat. I also remembered when

---

[1] MotivAider® is a registered trademark of Behavioral Dynamics, Inc.

I watched a really sharp consultant give a presentation at our division meeting yesterday. Oh yeah, there were also a few times that something made me think about my career, and when I did, I remembered to stop slouching."

"So whenever something reminds you of your intention to improve your posture, you straighten up. Is that right?"

"Sure I do. And I'm sure that if there were enough things like that happening to keep me thinking about my posture, I'd have the problem licked. I know that what allowed me to finally stay on track in coaching my staff is that I created enough reminders to keep my intention on the front burner. I could probably think of some ways to remind myself to straighten my back once in a while. But I can't see how I could possibly create enough reminders to actually solve my slouching problem. I mean, I slouch all the time. It's a habit. And it's going to take lots and lots of reminders for me to change it."

"David," I asked, "do you think this would help? What if I were to become your 'posture coach.' I'd follow you around all day long, every day. Every few minutes, I'd tap you gently on the shoulder and whisper in your ear, 'David, keep your back straight.' "

"Yeah," David said, chuckling, "I'm sure that would do the trick. But that's not very practical, is it?"

"Not exactly," I replied. "But I think we can come awfully close."

At this point, I introduced David to a follow through tool I invented called the MotivAider®.

"David," I said as I showed him a compact device that looks like a beeper, "here's your coach-to-go. It's called a MotivAider. It was designed to help people use Spotlighting. Its job is to keep reminding you of what you intend to do so that your intention won't get lost in the shuffle. It's especially useful when the only reason you're not following through is that there aren't enough of the right cues out there to keep your mind focused on your intention."

"How does it work?" David asked.

"Well, it's pretty simple. All it does is periodically send you a private signal—a gentle, silent vibration. The vibration does two things. First, it gets your attention. Second, it carries a personal message. It's a message that you devise yourself to remind and motivate you to do what you intend to do."

"Let's say, David, that you choose the message, 'Straighten up.' As you begin to use the MotivAider, you simply tell yourself that whenever you feel the vibration, you'll think 'Straighten up.' Soon, in the same way that the message, 'Someone is calling,' pops into your mind whenever you hear the phone ring, the message, 'Straighten up,' will pop into your mind whenever you feel the MotivAider vibrate. In other words, the vibration becomes a reminder or a cue for straightening your back.

"After you've turned the MotivAider's vibration into a personal cue, you simply set the device to automatically send you your cue as often as you choose. Then you just clip the MotivAider on your belt or waistband or slip it into a pocket. What you end up with is a steady stream of your own personal reminders flowing through your mind to keep you tuned in to your goal of improving your posture. You'll be exposed to enough of the right cues regardless of what's going on around you. There's no way that you'll forget to straighten your back."

David seemed intrigued but somewhat skeptical.

"It's a little hard to believe that something this simple will help me solve a problem that I've been unable to solve for years," he said. "On the other hand, it sure does make sense.

"I do have an idea for a personal message that might work better for me, though. How about, 'I'm no slouch'? That'll give me a little extra push because it'll remind me of the reason

why I want to solve my posture problem. It'll certainly tune
me in to the right voice."

"Sounds great," I said.

Spotlighting Gets Results

When he came back a month later, David was excited. His
experiment in MotivAider-assisted Spotlighting had worked
beautifully.

"I set the MotivAider to signal me every five minutes,"
David reported. "Whenever I felt the MotivAider vibrate, the
message, 'I'm no slouch,' popped into my mind just the way
you said it would. I would then check to see if my back was
straight, and if it wasn't, I fixed it. Before long, my posture
was good nearly every time I checked it. And within a couple
of weeks, keeping my back straight had become a habit. I did
it just as automatically as I used to slouch."

David had once again used Spotlighting successfully. He
used cues to keep himself tuned in to a voice that urged him
to behave in accord with his intention.

David went on to use Spotlighting on his own to resurrect
and successfully follow through with a number of other intentions that had earlier withered on the vine. Thanks to his
newfound understanding of cues, David was able, for example,
to finally keep his home office organized; to finally react to his
hyperactive son the way he believed he should instead of the
way his emotions pushed him to; and to finally put into practice
some ideas he had had for years on how to improve his ability
as a presenter.

When David's sister, Candace, complained to David about
how angry she was with herself for always getting into arguments with their elderly mother, David wondered out loud
whether Spotlighting might help. After he explained what Spot-

lighting was and how he had used it, Candace was eager to give it a try.

"I know exactly which voice I need to tune in to whenever I go to visit Mom," Candace told David. "It's the voice that knows that getting along with her is more important than being right. I know that in my soul, David. But I always seem to think of it only *after* I've gotten into a ridiculous argument with Mom and she's already in tears."

David helped Candace create cues to tune her in to the right voice. After considering and dismissing a number of possibilities, Candace shouted, "I've got it!" She decided that the incessant chatter of her mother's lovebirds would do the trick. "It's perfect. They actually sound like they're bickering," Candace told David. "From now on, whenever I hear those birds, it'll remind me that getting along with Mom is more important than being right."

David told us that his sister was doing quite well with Spotlighting, although she had recently gotten into a big fight with her mother when she made a surprise visit to Candace's house. "Without those lovebirds," Candace told David, "I'm lost."

We asked David and several others who had mastered the master strategy of Spotlighting to draw on their personal experience to help us generate a collection of observations, discoveries and nuggets of advice to help our clients and readers understand and harness the power of cues.

Here's what they came up with:

—I've learned that a good intention won't work unless I can find a way to keep it on the front burner. That's just the way it is.

—I've learned that cues have a much greater effect on me than I ever imagined. I used to think that I was totally in charge of how I behaved. Was I ever wrong! As a result of learning the truth, now I really am in charge. That's

because I use cues on purpose to keep me on track. Now
I even set my computer to automatically remind me of
my intentions—not just my schedule and specific tasks.
—They say you are what you eat. I've learned that, to a
large extent, you are the cues around you. I now watch
my cues as carefully as I watch my diet. When I notice
that I'm not acting the way I've decided I should, I ask
myself if I need to change my cue "diet."
—The folks on Madison Avenue know all about cues. They
bombard us with cues all the time to influence us to buy
the products they market. I've learned to watch and learn
from how they do it. They're good at it! For example, I
realize that I bought the car I did largely because of the
ads I saw that stirred up my worries about my family's
safety. Safety's always been important to me, but without
the ads, it certainly wouldn't have been on the top of my
list of requirements. Interestingly, the car I bought before
this one had an awful safety record. I bought it, I'm sure,
because the advertising stirred my remaining adolescent
interest in turning heads.
—I've learned that when I do follow through, it's probably
because there are cues out there that are helping me. I
make a point of looking for them and learning from them.
I noticed, for example, that I'm still pursuing a business
idea I had because my friends are always expressing interest in the idea and keep asking me how my research is
going.
—When I'm not following through, I've learned to stop and
ask myself the right questions. First I ask, "Are there
enough cues out there urging me to do what I should
do?" Then I ask, "Are there too many of the wrong cues
out there urging me to do what I shouldn't do?" The
answers usually point me in the direction of a solution.
—I've learned that it's hard to follow through when you're

surrounded by the wrong cues. Take it from me, a gour-
met deli is not the place to work if you want to stick to
a diet! You should see how good I am about eating when
I'm at the health spa, though. You'd think I was a different
person.

—I've learned how to make my own cues. I put notes and
reminders everywhere that I'm likely to stumble across
them. As soon as I start ignoring a particular reminder,
I look for a new way to get it right in my face. I don't
want my reminders to just sit there. I want them to jump
right out at me like a jack-in-the-box. I think my most
creative cue so far is the one I use first thing in the morning
to remind myself to slow down. I keep a big fat rubber
band around my comb. As I remove the rubber band each
day to use the comb, I think, "Whoa! This isn't a race."

—I've learned that my mother was right all along. Don't
hang around with the wrong crowd! People are cues too.
I've noticed that being around certain people helps me
follow through; being around other people has a negative
effect. I've learned to choose my company carefully when
I'm working on a good intention.

—I've learned not to ask why. Sometimes I have no idea
why certain cues have the effect that they have on me.
But if they help, who cares, I stay around them. And if
they hurt, I try to get as far away from them as I can.
I've discovered, for example, that when I go to the mall,
I spend my money more sensibly if I'm wearing high heel
shoes! I have no idea why. But now, whenever I need to
curb my spending, I don't ask any questions. I just put
on my heels.

—I've learned how to be very systematic about cues and
voices. Whenever I have a new intention, I start out by
making a list of all the voices that could help me follow
through and a list of all the voices that could lead me

astray. Next, I try to identify cues that will stimulate the helpful voices and cues that will stimulate the unhelpful ones. Then I look for ways to get exposed to as many of the helpful cues as possible and as few of the unhelpful ones as possible.

How Your Imagination Can Help You
Follow Through

What does using your imagination have to do with following through? Possibly a great deal.

A vivid imagination can allow you to correct for your hardwired tendency to be less affected by what's *down the road and uncertain* than by what's *definitely in your face right now.* With a good imagination used effectively, you can make the iffy, longer-term benefits of following through—or the hazards of not following through—feel real.

Say you're working on a book. You intend to write after supper, but when the time comes, you just can't get yourself to sit down and work. What if suddenly a picture pops into your mind? There you are accepting the Pulitzer Prize for the bestseller you wrote. The picture is so clear, so sharp, and so real that you can actually feel the pride and satisfaction that you earned with your hard work and persistence. It's a delicious feeling—a feeling that motivates you to get to work.

The very best athletes and super high achievers know all about it: If it's vivid and compelling enough, what you imagine can be as powerful as what's real. Serious daydreaming about the ultimate rewards of following through—or the ultimate costs of not following through—can bring you a motivating taste of the future.

But most of us can't count on our imagination to *automatically* help us follow through. It takes some work to turn your imagination into a powerful follow through asset. First, you have to be able to deliberately conjure up a clear mental picture that makes you *feel* like doing what you intend to do—a picture that leaves you with no doubt that following through is worth the trouble. Next, you have to use Spotlighting to make sure that there are enough cues out there to *keep* reminding you to conjure up that motivating picture. Without this second step, your imagination won't do you much good.

Combine your imagination with Spotlighting and you've got yourself a winning follow through team. You'll be able to keep your mind filled with the same kind of motivating pictures that help champion achievers make their daydreams come true.

CHAPTER 12

Master Strategy #2: Willpower Leveraging

Little strokes, fell great oaks.

—Benjamin Franklin

While approaching his car in the parking lot, Frank Lee Clueless noticed that one of the rear tires was flat. He was upset. He tried to calm himself down. "I can change this tire. I'm in good shape," he told himself. "People change tires all the time. I should be able to do it too." So Frank, who was indeed a strong man, went over to the trunk of his car where the spare tire and jack were stored. He took out the spare tire and laid it on the ground next to the flat. Then he closed the trunk, knelt down, and reached under the rear bumper with both hands. With all his might, he tried to lift up the car. Had he been able to do it, he was planning to hold the car up on one knee and then reach over and loosen the lug nuts with his fingers.

After fifteen minutes of huffing, puffing, and straining, Frank gave up. He was exhausted and demoralized. "Other people change tires all the time. Why can't I do it? I must be a real weakling," he thought.

Frank was no weakling. But he was being awfully foolish. Why would anybody try to change a tire by lifting a car with their bare hands? By trying to do things the hard way, Frank couldn't get the job done even though he had plenty of strength.

Of course the right way to change a tire is to do it the smart way, that is, by using the right tools. A tire jack allows you to get a big result out of a small amount of physical strength. It will enable a ninety-pound weakling to lift a three-thousand-pound vehicle off the ground and keep it there as long as it takes to change the tire. It's simply a matter of leverage.

Working Smarter

Without even realizing it, people every day "do it the hard way" when it comes to following through. Like Frank, they rely on brute force alone—on their willpower—to get the job done.

Enter the second follow through Master Strategy, Willpower Leveraging. In the same way that a tire jack increases what you can accomplish with the physical strength you have, Willpower Leveraging increases what you can accomplish with the willpower you have.

Willpower Leveraging means taking one easy action *today* that makes it much more likely that you'll do the right thing *tomorrow*.

This plot from an old low-budget movie should give you a good feel for what Willpower Leveraging is all about:

A father and his young son were taking a long hike in the woods. All of a sudden, a werewolf jumped out of the brush, bit the father's leg, and disappeared again into the forest. The father, who knew all about werewolves, was alarmed but remained clearheaded. He realized that as a result of the bite, he himself would soon become a werewolf. What's more, he realized that, as a werewolf, he would have an irresistible urge to attack the first human he saw, which of course would be his own precious son.

The father had an idea. He took his son by the hand and rushed to a nearby spot in the woods where there was a large cage that had been abandoned long ago by trappers. He immediately got into the cage, slammed the door shut, and using the rusty padlock that had been left dangling on the door latch, he locked himself in.

"Now when I turn into a werewolf," he explained to his bewildered son, "I won't be able to harm you, no matter how strong the urge is."

The Werewolf Dad understood the master strategy of Willpower Leveraging. He knew that if he relied on his willpower alone, that his intention not to harm his son would be no match for the powerful primal urge he was about to feel. So he leveraged the willpower he had by locking himself in a cage. Realizing that it was about to become extremely difficult for him to follow through, he took one critical action now—when it was still relatively easy—that made it possible for him to behave in accord with his intention later on. Willpower Leveraging allowed him to accomplish what he never would have been able to accomplish by relying on willpower alone.

A Different Kind of Monster

Kent wasn't a werewolf, he was an accountant. But every evening, as he relaxed in front of the TV, he felt like a monster— a cookie monster, that is. It wasn't at all unusual for Kent to polish off half a box of chocolate chip cookies in an evening. And when he was done, he felt guilty, stupid, and fat.

Kent decided to begin a serious campaign to stop eating so many cookies. The campaign didn't go very well. He felt strong and confident during dinner. But as he sat and watched TV, his resolve would weaken. He could almost hear the cookies call his name from the kitchen. He tried to resist. He tried hard. But usually, after an hour or so of struggling to "be good," he would give in to his craving. He would then go to the kitchen to have "just one cookie." Four trips to the kitchen and nine or ten cookies later, Kent, feeling like a beached whale, would finally stop eating.

After about a week of progressively firmer promises and no follow through, Kent was ready to throw in the towel. "I'm so disgusted with myself," he complained. "Any idiot would have enough willpower not to eat cookies. I can't believe that I'm such a wimp."

When Kent heard about Willpower Leveraging, it made sense to him. He quickly realized that all he had to do to solve his cookie-eating problem was to take one simple action: He asked his wife to stop buying cookies! She was happy to oblige.

Kent got a lot of "bang" for the "buck" of willpower it took to ask his wife for help. With no cookies in the house, whenever he felt the urge to eat cookies, the thought of driving six miles to the grocery store at that time of night was a big enough hurdle to keep Kent cookie-free.

Kent was finally following through, not because he was working harder, but because he was working smarter. Relying on willpower alone had gotten him nowhere. By leveraging his willpower, he was able to get the job done.

Fido, the Incredible Follow Through Machine

Willpower Leveraging can take a variety of forms. For the Werewolf Dad, it meant taking an action now that made it impossible to do the wrong thing later. For Kent, it meant taking an action now that made it a hassle to do the wrong thing later. For Pete and Karen, Willpower Leveraging meant taking an action now that bombarded them later with irresistibly compelling reasons to do the right thing.

Pete and Karen had been struggling for some time to find a way to follow through on their intention to exercise regularly. They had tried everything. Pete joined a health club, but within just a few weeks, he stopped going. Karen tried getting up early to run before work, but within a few days, the only exercise she was getting was from hitting the snooze button on her alarm clock. They went out and bought an expensive piece of exercise equipment. They even put it right smack-dab in the middle of their bedroom so that they couldn't possibly forget about it. Within a month, the exercise machine had become an extremely expensive clothes hanger.

Then one night, after lamenting about how they just didn't seem to have enough willpower to stick with anything, Pete and Karen stumbled upon the perfect solution: "Let's get a dog!" they decided.

Thanks to one easy action—adopting an adorable puppy named Casey from the animal shelter—Pete and Karen now get up early and walk every single day. They do it even when they'd rather sleep; even when the weather stinks; even when getting out of bed and going for a walk is the last thing in the world they feel like doing.

Pete and Karen don't get regular exercise because it's healthy. They get it because, now that they have Casey, getting up and getting exercise feels like a necessity rather than just a good—but optional—idea. They get up and go for a walk because Casey whines to go out; because they don't want him to start barking and wake up the neighbors; because they don't want him to make a mess on the carpet; and because they love Casey and don't want him to be uncomfortable.

So, for all the "wrong" reasons, Pete and Karen are finally doing what they were unable to do for all the "right" reasons. They're finally getting the job done because they discovered leverage and stopped relying on willpower alone.

The Moment of Truth

Although we're sure that Napoleon never heard of Willpower Leveraging, he certainly understood the idea behind it.

Napoleon discovered that the best way to get his soldiers to fight—and fight passionately—was to leave them with no choice. That's why he ordered his lieutenants to go back and burn the bridges that his troops had crossed on their way to meet the enemy. In other words, he made sure that they would move forward by making sure that they couldn't move backwards.

"Burning your bridges behind you" is the very heart and soul of Willpower Leveraging.

When you use Willpower Leveraging, you face a "moment of truth." This is the anxious point in time when you realize that, like the Werewolf Dad, you can choose to give up some freedom—you can burn a bridge—in order to lock yourself into following through. And once you've made the decision to burn a bridge, anxiety usually gives way to a great sense of relief. As one bridge-burner put it, "It's out of my hands now. Sure I've lost some freedom. But the freedom I lost was the freedom I had been using to do the wrong thing! Now I'm locked in to doing the right thing. What a relief!"

Do You Really Need to Lock Yourself in a Cage?

It's rarely feasible to completely burn your bridges behind you. Fortunately, however, seldom is it necessary. You usually don't have to make it *impossible* to go backwards. You just have to make it *difficult enough*. Instead of burning bridges, you have to pile large enough obstacles on them.

When Kent asked his wife to stop bringing home cookies, for example, he put a medium-sized obstacle on the bridge. He made an educated guess that having to get in his car and drive several miles at night just to get cookies would be a large enough obstacle to keep him from retreating. Had it turned out that he was wrong, instead of giving up, he could have just gone back and placed a larger obstacle on the bridge. For example, he could have asked his daughter to park behind his car in the driveway every evening so that, on top of the obstacle of having to drive several miles to get cookies, he could have stacked the obstacle of having to ask his daughter, who was already giving him a hard time about his "cookie-belly," to move her car so that he could go "Um . . . pick up something at the store." And if that didn't do the trick, he could have gone further yet. He could, for example, have had his wife hide his car keys every night.

The point is, there are lots of options between the extremes of keeping your bridges wide open and burning them completely. The trick is to make an educated guess about what it will take to keep you from retreating. Choose an obstacle and give it a try. If it doesn't work, don't stop there. Build on the obstacle or replace it with a bigger one. Keep experimenting until you're moving forward.

Reactions to Willpower Leveraging

We asked several people we worked with to draw on their experience to give you a livelier feel for the benefits of using Willpower Leveraging. Here's what they reported:

—I'd say that my life has been simpler and my mind less cluttered since I learned how to use Willpower Leveraging. I used to waste lots of time and mental energy struggling to make and carry out a bunch of individual decisions when one decision was really all it would have taken. I had decided, for example, to start saving money regularly. I figured that two hundred dollars a month would be about right. At the end of every month, I'd start to think about saving. I covered the same ground month after month after month. I'd always come to the same conclusion—that I should put away two hundred dollars—but getting it done was such a hassle that sometimes I just skipped it. Willpower Leveraging made all the difference in the world. I took just one action—I made one trip to the bank and told them to transfer two hundred dollars from my checking account to my savings account on the last day of every month. I admit that I felt pretty nervous signing the papers. But then right after I did it, I felt relieved. Now I'm saving exactly the way I always thought I should. Plus, there's a big bonus. It's off my mind! That one decision automatically took care of everything. It's not a burden anymore.

—I've learned that a little willpower applied at the right time can do wonders. I love everything about my favorite restaurant, except for the huge portion of delicious, crispy french fries they serve with their sandwiches. Actually, I love the fries. *That* was the problem! Even though I would set out every time to eat "only a few," I would end up eating every single one of those fries every single time. Although they were delicious, I felt lousy about what I was doing. Then, one day, on the way to the restaurant, I had an idea: When I order my sandwich, I'll just say, "Hold the fries." So that's what I did. Although it took just a little bit of willpower to say those three simple words, doing it accomplished a lot. As the waiter left my table, I found myself letting out a great sigh of relief. I knew that I would be spared from the usual struggle. I knew that instead of needing massive amounts of will-power to fight—and still lose—about fifty individual bat-tles with fifty irresistibly scrumptious french fries, just by saying "Hold the fries," I had won the whole war in one fell swoop! Hey, it might not sound like much, but Willpower Leveraging improved my lunch, my day, and my outlook. I felt like I was finally in control. And now that the waiter automatically asks me, "Should I hold the fries?" it's gotten even easier!

—Willpower Leveraging has really helped me deal with the problem of avoidance. I used to waste tons of time and energy avoiding things that, even though they were really important, just felt too difficult to do. I hoped they would get easier if I just waited long enough, but they only got harder. And as a result, not only did I fail to reap the benefits of following through with those things, but I spent lots of time fretting about them.

Take public speaking, for example. I've known for years that it would help my career a lot if I could give a good speech, but it's always terrified me. To get over my fear, I kept promising myself that the next time I heard about an opportunity to speak, I would volunteer. But whenever an opportunity came along, I felt paralyzed.

Although a part of me wanted to jump right in, another part of me wanted to run and hide. So instead of volunteering right away, I would put it off, hoping I would muster up enough courage to go ahead. But with each passing day, instead of getting more courage, I just got more scared. The bottom line is that I never did step up to the plate, even though I was frustrated with myself for just sitting on the sidelines.

Willpower Leveraging helped me see that when I'm avoiding something important but scary, the key is to burn my bridges immediately, because the longer I wait, the more I'll want to retreat. In other words, my desire to avoid gets stronger the closer I get to D-Day. So the earlier I can commit myself, the better.

So now when I hear about an opportunity to speak, I say "yes" right away, before the idea of actually speaking becomes real enough and scary enough to make me want to avoid it. That way, when reality sets in—and it always does—it's already too late for me to back out no matter how much I feel like doing just that. I'm stuck, and that's exactly where I want to be. And it's working great. Although public speaking still isn't my favorite thing to do, I'm getting pretty good at it as a result of all the practice. And it turns out I was right about one thing all along: It *is* helping my career.

—When I first learned about Willpower Leveraging, I used it to help me follow through on some really important things in my life. But what's been interesting to me is that now that I'm familiar with the strategy, I find myself using it quite often for little things. And I really get a kick out of how well it works.

For example, I recently used Willpower Leveraging to solve a problem with my exercise routine. I don't have any trouble getting myself to walk every morning, but I haven't been able to get myself to do upper-body exercise like lifting weights or doing push-ups. For one thing, I don't have the time, and for another, I find that kind of exercise boring.

On my way out for my walk the other morning, for some reason my eyes stumbled on the hand weights that had been sitting on the shelf for months, and suddenly I had an idea. "Just pick up the weights," I told myself. "Once you get out the door with the weights in your hands, you'll have to carry them the whole way. Just pick them up."

So I did.

My idea worked better than I expected. By the time I got back, my arm and shoulder muscles ached from all the exercise they'd gotten. I felt great about having, in effect, put one over on myself. It was so easy, it was actually amusing. By exerting one tiny bit of willpower, I had set things up so that I would get a half hour of good upper-body exercise. Since then, every morning on the way out the door, I grab the weights.

Are Your Promises Only Skin Deep?

"That's it," Gerald exclaimed, as he looked with disgust at the bulging balance on his credit card statement. "The time has come for me to get serious about curbing my spending." Gerald knew exactly what he needed to do. "It'll be nothing but necessities from now on— no frills until I get this bill paid off," he insisted. Gerald was serious. He knew it was the right thing to do. And he promised himself he would do it.

The phone rang. It was his friend, Dan.

"Dan, I've made a firm commitment to quit spending money on anything but necessities from now on," Gerald informed his friend. "This time, buddy, I'm really serious."

"Gerald," his friend asked, "are you really, *really* serious about this?"

"You bet I am," Gerald answered with no hesitation.

"Are you sure?" asked Dan.

"Absolutely positive," Gerald replied. "Please stop asking me if I'm sure. I AM SURE, okay?"

"Okay, Gerald. I'll tell you what," said Dan. "If you're really so sure, then why don't you just go ahead and secure your promise the way you secure a loan. We'll draw up some papers that say that unless you do what you've promised to do, you'll give me your car and that beer stein collection I've always been dying to get my hands on. I'm serious. Is it a deal?"

"Are you nuts?" snapped Gerald. "I'm not going to take a chance like that."

"A chance? What chance?" Dan asked, sounding puzzled. "I thought you said you were serious about your promise. Aren't you the only one who controls how you spend your money? How could you possibly be taking a chance if you're truly as serious about this as you say you are?"

Dan waited for Gerald's response.

"Gerald, are you still there?" asked Dan. "Gerald . . . Hello? . . . Gerald?"

CHAPTER 13

Creating Compelling Reasons

Although hard work may *pay off in the future, laziness* definitely *pays off now.*

—Anonymous

In this chapter, we'll introduce you to a follow through strategy that corrects for our hardwired tendency to be more heavily influenced by what *feels most real* at the moment than by what we *know* is important in the long run. First we'll review how this tendency causes follow through failures. Then we'll show you how you can use the very same tendency to create follow through successes.

Ray certainly intended to follow his doctor's recommendation. He realized how important it was to treat his high blood pressure. He knew that the medication his doctor prescribed would substantially reduce his chances of having a heart attack. Yet Ray quit taking his blood pressure medication. He didn't *decide* to quit taking it. He just quit. It wasn't because he didn't care. Ray was quite fond of living. He had a great job, a great family, a great life. He was happy and well-adjusted.

The fact is, Ray's behavior—like the behavior of the countless other patients who quit taking their medication long before they should—was influenced more by the immediate and certain inconvenience of taking a pill than by the more distant and less certain benefit of "possibly" prolonging the life he loved. The minor cost of following through—the bother of having to take a pill—felt more real and more compelling than the major benefit of following through—increasing his chances of living longer and healthier.

So Ray's health is now in jeopardy because all the "right" reasons for him to follow through don't have enough horsepower to get him up and over the minor but very real bother of taking pills.

The fact that we're wired to react more to what feels real at the moment than to what we know is important in the long run is usually bad news for good intentions. That's because intentions usually require us to do things that we don't really *feel* like doing.

But under the right circumstances, the way we're wired can actually help us follow through. It happens whenever we're in a situation that gives us a truly "compelling" reason—whether or not it's the "right" reason—to do the same thing we intend to do.

For years, Paul had counted on the right reason to get him to follow through on his intention to floss his teeth regularly. But because the right reason wasn't a compelling reason, his teeth remained unflossed.

Now Paul flosses all the time. Ask him if it's because he finally understands that good dental hygiene is important, and he'll answer, "Heck no! I've always understood that." But the understanding itself never made him feel enough like flossing to compel him to actually do it. The reason that Paul now flosses is that he now has large spaces between his teeth where food routinely gets stuck. "It's uncomfortable," he told us. "It drives me nuts until I can get the pieces of food out."

Paul learned that although he hadn't been able to do the right thing for the *right* reason, he was able to do the right thing for the *wrong* reason. The key is to have a compelling reason—a reason he could really feel—for doing the right thing. The compelling reason for him to floss is to get relief from the uncomfortable feeling he has when there's food stuck between his teeth. That reason *moves* him; the right reasons he had counted on for years took him nowhere. "If I had had bigger spaces between my teeth years ago," Paul told us, "I know I would have taken much better care of my teeth all along!"

Rebecca learned about the power of compelling reasons while she was struggling to stick to a diet.

On her way to her neighbor Sally's home to drop off a package that had been delivered to Rebecca by mistake, Rebecca thought about what a wonderful cook Sally was.

As Rebecca got ready to ring the doorbell, she gave herself a speech. "Sally's probably going to offer me something delicious to eat. But I'm not happy with how sloppy I've been lately about my diet. I can't stand how fat I'm getting. If Sally offers me something fattening, I'm just going to have to say no. That's all there is to it."

As Rebecca handed the package to Sally and began to explain what had happened, Sally interrupted her. "Why don't you come on in, dear, and try a piece of my special green apple pie? Your timing is wonderful. I think it's just about ready to come out of the oven."

"I'd really love to," Rebecca replied, "but I can't. I'm on a diet."

"Are you sure, dear? This is my best pie recipe ever.

It's so much work, I make it only once a year. But if I do say so myself, it's out of this world," Sally pleaded.

"Well, it smells delicious," said Rebecca, knowing that she should just say No and stick with it. But as the fragrance enveloped her, she began to weaken. "Maybe I could have just a small piece," Rebecca thought to herself. "After all, this is a special pie. And I can always have a light supper tonight to make up for it."

Just as Rebecca, her mouth watering, was about to surrender, Sally added, "You know, dear, there's a secret ingredient in this pie that makes it taste so good. You'd never guess what it is from the taste, but somehow it just works magic with the other ingredients."

"What is it?" asked Rebecca, getting ready to follow Sally into the kitchen.

"It's tomato paste!"

Suddenly Rebecca, who just a minute earlier was all set to abandon her intention, had all the willpower in the world. Now she had a truly compelling reason to stick to her diet. And as a result, she had gone in a flash from an "I really shouldn't but I will anyway," to a rock solid, "Absolutely, positively no way."

You see, although Rebecca loved tomatoes, they hated her. She was allergic to them. Very allergic. Eating the tiniest bit would cause her to instantly break out in an ugly itchy rash, swell up like a blowfish, and then be left with a throbbing headache that would wipe her out for at least two days.

So this time, when Rebecca said, "I can't," she didn't.

Although the "right" reasons for sticking to her diet couldn't get her up and over her lively desire to eat some of Sally's yummy pie, Rebecca now had a *compelling* reason to do what she intended to do all along. She could really feel, not just think, "Eating this pie will mean big, big trouble for me." And that feeling was powerful enough to cause her to stick like glue to her diet.

In reflecting on her encounter with the tomato-tainted pie, Rebecca chuckled, "I should probably sprinkle tomato flakes on everything I've decided not to eat. That way I'd stick to my diet for sure!"

Hmm.

Little did Rebecca know that her tongue-in-cheek idea, although impractical, was a fine illustration of an extremely powerful follow through strategy: Deliberately creating a compelling reason to follow through.

Doing It on Purpose

It's quite a simple idea: When the "right" reasons aren't compelling enough to get you to follow through, then deliberately create a reason that *is*—one that you can really feel; one that moves you to do the same thing you intend to do.

Deliberately creating a compelling reason to follow through lets you take a common "cause" of poor follow through—the powerful hardwired tendency to be unduly influenced by what feels most real at the moment—and turn it into a "cure" for poor follow through.

Mary Poppins had the right idea when she sang, "Just a spoonful of sugar helps the medicine go down." Rebecca had the right idea too, only she came at it from a different angle. For her, it was "Just a spoonful of 'poison' keeps the 'sugar' from going down!"

But it was Jeff, an insurance agent, who hit the nail right on the head. "If I know I should 'scratch,' " he told us after he had mastered the art of creating compelling reasons, "I try to figure out a way to make myself 'itch.' In other words, I set things up so that I'll actually *feel* like doing what I know I should do."

When we first met Jeff, he didn't have a clue about why he had been failing so miserably to keep a promise he had made to himself a year ago.

After attending a sales conference, Jeff made a commitment to himself to make ten cold calls a week to prospective clients. He had what he considered to be an excellent reason to follow through. He was convinced that making the calls would help him achieve his financial goals. But somehow the right reasons just weren't getting him up and over the very real bother of doing what he intended to do.

We first helped Jeff understand why the right reasons didn't have enough horsepower to compel him to follow through. Jeff certainly "knew" that there was a connection between making cold calls *now* and improving his financial condition *in the future*. What he didn't realize, though, was that *knowing* that there's a connection isn't the same as *feeling* the connection. There was never a moment when Jeff could actually feel in his gut that making a cold call right now would bring him the success he wanted. Neither was there a moment when he could actually feel in his gut that he would lose something if he didn't make a call.

There were three obstacles that prevented Jeff from intensely feeling the connection between doing (or not doing) what he intended to do and the results.

First, what Jeff stood to gain (or lose) was just too far off in the future to feel real to him. Without any way to "taste" the results of his action or inaction right now—or at least darn soon—the right reasons for following through were not about to move him.

Second, the connection between following through and benefiting (or not following through and losing something) were less than airtight. There was too much uncertainty, too much slack—too much of what we call "wiggle room" between what he did (or didn't) do and what he would gain (or lose). There was no guarantee that making each dreaded call would pay off; neither was there any guarantee that Jeff's failure to make a call would cost him anything.

Third, although Jeff certainly wanted to earn more money, he was already doing okay financially. His intention was based on a genuine desire to improve his financial condition, but it wasn't an especially lively desire. It didn't feel much like an itch—not the way it did a few years ago when Jeff was on pins and needles every month when the house payment was due and his second child was on the way.

Once Jeff understood why the right reasons weren't working, he had a basis for creating a compelling reason to follow through on his good intention.

He realized that he would have to create a reason that brought the benefits of following through (or the costs of not following through) close enough so that he could *feel* them instead of just *thinking* them. If the impact on his financial future didn't move him, then maybe an impact on his financial present would.

Jeff also knew that he had to find a way to eliminate the wiggle room. He realized that he disliked making cold calls so much that if there was any chance at all that it didn't really matter if he made them or not, he surely wouldn't bother. So besides being close up, the gains and losses would have to be *certain*. Each and every time he did the right thing, it would have to be worth his while; each and every time he failed to do the right thing, it would have to cost him something.

Finally, Jeff understood that in order to move him, a reason to follow through would have to fit who he was. It would have to really matter to him. Although he wanted to believe that the promise of "sugar" would move him, he knew himself better than that. Not that Jeff didn't want more sugar. But his "hunger" for more was less than ravenous. On the other hand, Jeff was frugal to a fault. He couldn't stand the thought of wasting his own money. Surely the threat of "poison"—losing money he already had—would get Jeff in gear.

So here's the follow through plan that Jeff devised and that his assistant, Dawn, helped him implement.

From now on, when Dawn makes her weekly trips to the bank to make deposits, she'll get a hundred dollars in cash—ten ten-dollar bills to be exact. She'll put the money, which belongs to Jeff, in an envelope marked "Jeff's Cold Calls" and keep the envelope in a locked drawer in her desk. At the end of each day, Dawn will ask Jeff if he made any cold calls that day and, if so, how many.

For each call Jeff made, Dawn will remove one ten-dollar bill from the envelope and give it back to him. Finally, every Friday afternoon at four o'clock, if there's any money left in the envelope, Dawn will call Jeff to her desk and have him watch while she feeds the remaining tens to an obliging paper shredder.

Ouch!

Jeff had no trouble making ten cold calls every week. He still disliked making then. And he still wasn't moved by the right reasons. But he made the calls anyway because he now had a *compelling* reason to make them: he wanted to keep his own money out of the shredder.

Jeff had managed to set things up so that the only way he could get relief from the very real, immediate, and unpleasant threat of losing his money was to make "those damned calls." In other words, he succeeded in deliberately creating an "itch" that could only be "scratched" by doing the same thing that he intended to do all along.

The strategy of deliberately creating compelling reasons isn't just for pursuing financial and career goals. It can be used to rescue any intention that's languishing because the right reasons don't have enough horsepower.

Let's look at how Barb used the strategy to follow through on her intention to stay away from her abusive former boyfriend, Doug.

Although she'd concluded long ago that Doug was bad news for her, she found it extremely hard to follow through because she was terribly lonely and still attracted to him. As her sister Sherry put it, "She's addicted."

Frustrated with the failure of all the right reasons to keep her away from Doug, Barb asked her sister for help. "Sherry, please, promise you'll do this for me. From now on, whenever you see me, I want you to ask me if I've been with Doug. If I have—and you know I'll always tell you the truth—then I want you to call Dad right away and tell him what I did."

Barb responded to the look of horror on her sister's face. "No, Sherry, I haven't gone off the deep end. I've thought this through and I know exactly what I'm doing. You know how disappointed Dad will be if he hears that I've had anything at all to do with Doug again. And you know how I hate the thought of disappointing Dad. I think that just knowing that I can't see Doug anymore without Dad finding out about it will help me stay away from Doug."

Sherry agreed to help. When Barb had a slip about three weeks after putting the plan into action, Sherry did exactly what she was supposed to do. Their father reacted as predicted, and so did Barb. She never slipped again.

By depending on the right reasons to follow through, Barb had gotten nowhere. Now, for the compelling "wrong" reason that she had created on purpose, she was finally following through.

How To Create Compelling Reasons

Creating Compelling Reasons is more of an art than a science. Although there's no exact recipe, there are three common ingredients.

1. Make It Matter Now

The most compelling reasons bring you immediate results for doing (or failing to do) what you intend to do.

Results that come immediately or very soon will move you more than results that are further down the road. The threat of losing a finger right now, for example, will probably move you more than the threat of losing an arm way off in the future; the promise of a great meal this evening will probably move you more than the promise of a month's worth of great meals two years from now.

Take a lesson from our friends on Madison Avenue, whose prosperity depends on influencing us to buy stuff whether we really need it or not. They certainly understand and capitalize on the tendency we have to be influenced far more by what we expect to happen *sooner* than by what we expect to happen *later*. Just think about how often advertising messages promise pleasure now and defer the pain until later.

2. Eliminate Wiggle Room

The most compelling reasons have no wiggle room. The more certain—the tighter, the more guaranteed—the connection between doing the right thing and getting results, the greater the impact a reason for following through will have on your behavior.

If you're not convinced, just think about it. How often would you exceed the speed limit, get too close to the car in front of you, or park illegally, if you were absolutely certain you'd get a ticket *every time?* Would you eat rare beef, neglect to wash your hands, skip your daily vitamin, if you were absolutely certain you'd have a health crisis every time you did? Wouldn't you be more likely to take a pass on that chocolate donut if you were absolutely certain it would show as plain as day on your waistline? Wouldn't you read the newspaper the way you intended to if you were absolutely certain you'd lose five IQ points if you didn't? Wouldn't you get today's paperwork done, clean up the mess on your desk, or remember to thank your assistant for a job well done if you were absolutely certain that doing these things would guarantee that you'd get the promotion you want?

3. Make Sure It Fits You

The most compelling reasons are reasons that fit who you are—reasons that work hand in hand with what makes you tick.

When you set out to create a compelling reason, forget about what "they" say should be important; forget about what you only "think" should be important; and, by all means, forget about logic. Reasons that make the most sense may not move you at all. And reasons that do the best job of getting you up and running may not make much sense.

Be as honest as you can with yourself about what moves you. It doesn't have to be a "pretty" reason. And it doesn't have to have anything at all to do with the "right" reasons for following through.

If it moves you, it moves you; if it doesn't, it doesn't.

Sandy knows all about it, although she didn't actually have to create a compelling reason to quit smoking. Her husband "accidentally" did it for her.

Sandy "should have" quit smoking because smoking was bad for her health. That would have made sense. The reason she finally did quit, however, was far less sensible and far less important than that.

What finally moved Sandy up and over her addiction to cigarettes was her intense desire to put egg all over the face of her smart-aleck husband, Sid. "Not only did Sid have no confidence in my ability to quit, he seemed to take great delight in telling our friends that I didn't have enough willpower to do it," she explained. "His attitude really ticked me off. You can call me petty or childish or immature or even sick. But the fact of the matter is, embarrassing the hell out of my husband was a thrill worth suffering for! And although the urge to smoke is still pretty strong at times, I'd never give my husband the satisfaction of being right."

How Far Can You Go?

Once you grasp that you can create a truly compelling reason to follow through on virtually any intention, you may get a little nervous. It's the kind of nervous that comes from owning a powerful weapon. "How far dare I go?" you might ask. Is it going too far, for example, to offer to sign over your house and car to the stranger at the next table if you eat the brownie that you've promised yourself you won't eat?

We can't answer that question for you. What we can say with considerable confidence, however, is that if you did make such an offer, you wouldn't eat the brownie! If you're willing to unleash the potential power of compelling reasons, we dare say you can follow through on virtually any good intention you have.

Necessity Is the Mother of Follow Through

When I was starting my sports psychology business in 1989, I (Pete) hired a coach to help me get started. He urged me to develop a specialty niche that I could use to earn a reputation and spread my name. After some research, we decided that basketball free throw shooting was the perfect niche for me.

One day my coach, Rob, gave me an assignment. "Pete," he said matter-of-factly, "I want you to interview John Wooden about free throw shooting. And I want you to do it today."

I was flabbergasted. John Wooden is to basketball what Ronald Reagan is to the Republican party—a revered elder statesman, perhaps the best basketball coach of all time. "I can't call John Wooden," I pleaded.

"Do it," Rob said. "If you're serious about being successful in this business, do it. And do it today."

"Okay, I'll do it," I said.

"Good luck. I'll talk to you tomorrow," Rob said, hanging up quickly enough to give me no chance to back out.

I was so nervous about calling John Wooden that I did absolutely everything I could think of to avoid it. But every time I got close to deciding not to call, I thought of Rob and the promise I'd made. Rob was a great coach. But forgiving he wasn't. How could I possibly face him the next day and tell him that I hadn't kept my promise?

"That's it," I finally snapped at myself. "Pete, pick up the phone and dial the damned number." I started to dial. As I listened to the phone ringing on the other end, I remember praying, "God, I hope no one answers."

"Hello," a male voice answered.

"Is John Wooden there?" I asked nervously, hoping he wasn't. "Speaking," the voice on the other end replied.

My heart rate, which was already pretty fast, suddenly doubled. But after tripping over my tongue for a couple of minutes, I settled down. We spoke for forty-five minutes. It was great!

I got off the phone feeling like I had done the impossible. I felt like I had won a championship game.

As it turned out, making that one phone call changed my life. It did great things for my career and my confidence.

What enabled me to do it? It wasn't because my career meant everything to me. And it wasn't because I have so much willpower. I know in my heart that what enabled me to make that fateful call was that I just couldn't bear the thought of having to tell Rob that I'd chickened out.

CHAPTER 14

Leading the Horse to Water

The beginning is the most important part of the work.

—Plato

"Apparently, young man, you just don't like going to school," said the principal as he examined Brad's attendance record.

"That's not exactly true, sir," replied Brad. "I don't mind *going* to school. I just don't like what I have to do once I get there. If all I had to do was *go*, I'd go every day."

In the previous chapter, we introduced you to a follow through strategy that works by adding raw power to your intentions. In this chapter, we'll introduce you to a kinder, gentler strategy—one that treats your intentions with patience and understanding. Called *Leading the Horse*, this strategy is ideal when you're reluctant to bring out the heavy artillery because you're not convinced that it's necessary, because you think it might do more harm than good, or because you're just, well, too nervous to mess with all that power.

Not Even a Thirsty Horse Will Drink if He's Not Near Water

The Leading the Horse strategy puts a new spin on the old saying, "You can lead a horse to water, but you can't make him drink."

It's true that you can't make a horse drink if he's not thirsty enough. On the other hand, if you want him to drink, it makes sense to lead him to water. If the horse is right there where the water is, he'll certainly be more likely to drink when he does get the slightest bit thirsty. In other words, leading the horse to water puts the horse *in a better position* to drink.

The Leading the Horse strategy lets you boost your chances of following through by putting you *in a better position* to do what you intend to do.

Harry, the manager of a busy restaurant, could have used the Leading the Horse strategy to follow through on his intention to ride his exercise bike regularly. Instead, the only muscles that got any exercise were his "avoidance muscles."

It was the same scene night after night. There was Harry sitting in front of the TV with his favorite snack. "I really have to ride that bike tonight," he would remind himself. "Doc says I need aerobic exercise at least three times a week. So I should get on that bike right now. And just as soon as this next program is over, I will."

But as Harry watched TV, he couldn't help but think about the ordeal he was about to endure. He knew that in order to get any benefit, he would have to pedal and huff and puff and sweat for at least twenty minutes. "It's so boring that twenty minutes feels like a week," he complained. "I can hardly stand it. It's as bad as listening to Ted (one of Harry's least favorite customers) tell the same stories over and over and over again."

The more he thought about it, the deeper Harry would sink into his easy chair and the better the next TV program and the one after that would look to him. For Harry, the innocent-looking exercise bicycle had come to stand for torture.

Harry never really gave himself a chance to get into the habit of exercising regularly. That's because he had no idea that there was a simple, painless way to pave the way for doing what he knew he should do. All Harry knew was that the horse definitely wasn't thirsty—that he didn't want to pedal his exercise bike for twenty minutes. What Harry didn't realize was that he could just "lead the horse to water" without insisting that it drink; that he could just *sit* on the exercise bike each day without any obligation to pedal and huff and puff and sweat. What's more, he didn't realize that by just going to the water, he could increase the chances that he'd eventually drink.

Harry could have learned something from Brad the truant. Brad intuitively understood that "going" and "what you have to do once you get there," are really two separate matters. The first part is a piece a cake. The second part is a big spoonful of castor oil. The first part—going—is not only easy, it helps you follow through by taking you part of the way there. The second part—what you have to do once you get there—may be good for you, but it's definitely hard to swallow. The problem is, unless you separate the two parts, you make the whole thing worth avoiding.

An author who used the Leading the Horse strategy to finish writing an article she had been avoiding for months, put it this way: "It's like the difference between having to run up a steep hill and having only to stroll down a road that's level as far as you can see," she explained. "If I think I'll have to run up the hill, I usually don't even bother to get started. It just feels too hard. But if I tell myself that all I have to do is mosey on down the road and stop any time I feel like it, then off I go. And more often than not, by the time I get to the first hill, I've built up enough steam that I just keep right on going."

Because Harry didn't know about the Leading the Horse strategy, all he could see was the hill. All he could think about was how unpleasant it was going to be to ride the exercise bike for twenty minutes.

Had he known about the strategy, Harry would have taken a different approach. First, he would have asked himself: "When it comes to riding the exercise bike, how far down the road can I go before I hit the first hill?" His answer might have been, "I can go and sit on the bike, place my feet on the pedals, and pedal for ten seconds. I sure wouldn't mind doing that." If that was his answer, then that's all he would have required himself to do—nothing more.

But focusing so much on the hard part was what prevented Harry from going down the road at all. It kept him from building the momentum that would have helped him eventually make it up and over that hill. What Harry didn't realize was that sitting on the bike with his feet on the pedals would have put him in a much better position to go the distance—that is, to go ahead and do what he intended to do.

Woody Allen once said, "Eighty percent of success is showing up." The Leading the Horse strategy is 100 percent "showing up." It's separating the easy part of following through from the hard part, and then doing the easy part, *showing up,* so that you're in a better position to get the whole job done.

Jesse used the Leading the Horse strategy to follow through on his intention to clean the garage. For weeks, every time he thought about getting started, he could hear his soul moan. He would tell himself how important it was to get the job done, how much worse it would be if he kept putting it off, and how good he would feel if the garage wasn't such a mess. But all he accomplished by trying so hard to talk himself up and over his avoidance, was to make himself feel even worse about not following through.

Finally, Jesse wised up. "If all I intended to do was to put my grubby clothes on and go stand out in the garage, would I do it?"

"Sure I would," was his answer. "Why wouldn't I?" Then he asked, "What if I just added gathering up the few scattered paint cans and stacking them in the corner?" That felt okay to him too. But when he went just a little bit further and wondered if he would feel any reluctance if he added *organizing his tools* to his definition of showing up, he felt an unmistakable "No way" begin to form in his mind. So he immediately backed off. Showing up, he decided, would consist of nothing more than putting on his grubbies, going out to the garage, and stacking the paint cans.

How did it work? Well, the first time Jesse "showed up," before leaving the garage, he went ahead and gathered and stacked up some boxes, even though he didn't have to. The next weekend, he asked himself again what he could require himself to do without feeling any resistance at all. When he went out to the garage with an easy requirement in mind, he ended up spending two hours out there organizing. The next time he showed up, he again did only what he required himself to do and nothing more. The time after that, he really got into it. He spent about six hours, got the whole job done, and felt great about it.

Waiting for the Muse

Leading the Horse to Water is an ideal strategy to use when, instead of helping, pressure only interferes with doing what you intend to do. For example, if you're writing a novel and you've decided to require yourself to write five pages of beautiful, flowing, creative prose every day, you're making a big mistake. Insisting on creativity is probably the best way to squash it. Few writers can sit in front of a word processor and produce and express creative ideas at a consistent rate. There's usually lots of variability from day to day. One day you're hot, the next day you're not. The poet's muse comes and goes without warning. That's just the way it is. And requiring yourself to produce a certain quantity or quality of output will only guarantee that you'll produce a high enough level of frustration to undermine your writing ability and make writing worth avoiding.

Leading the Horse to Water lets you separate the easy, predictable part from the hard and unpredictable part of following through on your intention to keep working on your novel. You can require yourself, for example, to do nothing more than turn on your computer and sit in front of it for just a few minutes every day. If you show up and your muse shows up too, great. If you show up and your muse doesn't, oh well, you'll be back tomorrow for sure, and the next day and the day after that. If you're there every day ready to go, she'll show up sooner or later. If you require any more of yourself, get frustrated, and then stop showing up, you won't be there when your muse does come.

The Physics of Showing Up

If you're still not so sure that just showing up or "going" can help you "do what you have to do once you get there," maybe Nathan's description will convince you to at least give the Leading the Horse strategy a try. Nathan, a science teacher, had a wonderfully unique way of understanding just how and why the strategy worked for him.

I had been avoiding the job of assembling these booklets for weeks. The idea of having to punch holes in thirty twenty-six-page sets made me ill. I knew from experience that the hole punch would only handle a few pages at a time, that it would probably get jammed a few times, and that even if everything did go without a glitch, it would be a great challenge to stand there for an eternity and try to do this tedious, menial task without going completely bonkers.

When I learned about the Leading the Horse strategy, I was more than a little skeptical. But I figured I had nothing to lose. Besides, I was kind of intrigued with the idea of starting something knowing that I could bail out at any time.

So I told myself that I'd gather up what I needed, take it to the resource room, get it set up, and then pick up four or five pages and punch them. Then, unless I felt like doing any more, I'd call it a day.

To tell you the truth, considering how much I dreaded the job, I really didn't think I'd do any more than that. But once I got started, I felt like I might as well finish at least one booklet. So I did. Then, after reminding myself that I could stop at any time, I went ahead and did another one. When the second booklet was done, I just kept going and did another three booklets. When I got to the sixth booklet, I started to feel bored and restless. So I again reminded myself that I could stop at any time. I felt relieved. But then, instead of stopping, I collected some more sheets and started to punch again.

I remember thinking, "Oh well, I might as well get ten booklets done—a nice round number." Well, when the ten booklets were done, I kept going. While working on the eleventh booklet, I thought, "No sense stopping on an odd number, right?"

To make a long story short, I did all thirty booklets! It was amazing. Whenever I started to get sick of what I was doing, I just told myself, "No problem. I can stop right now if I want." And every time I realized that I was perfectly free to stop, I somehow chose to do just a little more before stopping.

When the job was all done, I remember smiling and shaking my head. "That was weird," I thought. It was just so strange that what allowed me to go ahead and do a job that I had been dreading and putting off for weeks was giving myself permission to quit at any time!

As I tried to explain to my fellow science teachers what had happened, I had this wonderful insight. I realized that my good intention to assemble those booklets had been like a space capsule circling the Earth.

With the "pull" of my desire to get the job done no stronger than the "push" of my desire to avoid doing something so tedious, my intention was stuck in orbit.

When I realized that I could quit whenever I felt like it, the idea of assembling the booklets felt a lot less repulsive to me. The "pull" to do it was finally greater than the "push" not to do it. It was like suddenly feeling gravity do its thing. Once I got started, I could actually *feel* myself being pulled by my desire to get the job done. I'll tell you, it was a psychology lesson I'll never forget!

Thank you, Nathan, for a physics lesson we'll never forget!

It doesn't matter whether you understand it best by considering the laws of physics, the challenge of getting a horse to drink, or the difference between going to school and staying there. All that matters is that the Leading the Horse strategy is a simple, gentle way to follow through on many of your good intentions.

To summarize, here are the basic steps:

1. Separate the easy, "Get started" part of what you intend to do from the hard, "Yuk, I don't want to do that" part.
2. Tell yourself that all you have to do is the easy part—that you can stop any time you want.
3. Go ahead and do the easy part.
4. Prepare yourself to be pleasantly surprised.

CHAPTER 15

Going Too Far

It is often easier to fight for one's principles than to live up to them.

—Adlai Stevenson

Tammy was a doughnut addict. She loved doughnuts. But she hated what they were doing to her waistline and her arteries. Although she intended to stay away from them, just about every day she'd give in to the temptation to have "just one" doughnut. Usually, after eating the one, she'd struggle for a while with the urge to eat "just one more," and then give in. On a typical day, she'd eat two or three doughnuts. But there were many days, Tammy confessed, when she had four or five. Her record high, she reported with embarrassment, was seven.

Tammy realized that her easy access to doughnuts at work was a big part of the problem. Unfortunately, though, there was nothing she could do to make them less accessible.

"I'm just one of fourteen people who work in my office," she told us. "My boss believes that having goodies available is good for morale. His assistant checks often to make sure that there are plenty of doughnuts left in the coffee room. If the supply gets low, she gets more doughnuts. So there's really no end to the amount of damage I can do."

Fortunately, there is a follow through strategy that you can use when you're in a predicament like Tammy's, that is, where you can't change a situation that's contributing to poor follow through. We call the strategy *Going Too Far*. It's a strategy that energizes an intention by essentially kicking sand in its face.

With the Going Too Far strategy, you don't have to fight the urge to do the wrong thing. Instead, all you have to do is make a deal with yourself.

Before we explain what kind of deal you have to make, get ready to ask, "Have these guys lost it?"

You see, the deal doesn't make intuitive sense. That's because it's not based on the sensible way you think the mind should treat good intentions. It's based on the nonsensical way that the mind actually does treat them.

So here's the deal: "If you're going to do the wrong thing, then you must do it even *wronger* than usual."

Going Too Far capitalizes on our discovery of a fascinating paradox:

You can make an intention more effective by threatening to violate it in a big way.

The strategy provokes intentions the way a motorist driving thirty miles an hour over the speed limit provokes a police officer to enforce the law even though the same police officer just ignored a dozen less serious violators.

We'll first show you how Tammy used Going Too Far to win the war against doughnuts. Then we'll explain why the strategy works and show you how you can use it to energize some of your own ineffective intentions.

"Tammy," we explained, "all you have to do is agree from now on that if you're going to eat any doughnuts at all, you must eat *three* doughnuts at a time. You can't eat just one any more. It's three or none at all. Can you agree to do that?"

"That sounds weird," she responded. "How will that help me gain control?"

"It'll work," we assured her, "as long as you're able to follow the 'three or none at all' rule without exception. If you're not able to stick with the rule, then this strategy won't work for you," we explained.

"I'm sure I can follow the rule," she said, "I obviously don't have any trouble eating doughnuts! It's just that it sounds awfully far-fetched to me. But if you think it'll work, I'm willing to give it a try."

Tammy tried the Going Too Far strategy and was pleasantly surprised.

"The very first day, I had the usual battle with temptation," she told us. "I finally surrendered and headed for the doughnuts. But when I got there and reached for one, I was surprised by what happened. Instead of feeling the usual anticipation and relief, I could feel my whole being rebel. 'I can't eat three doughnuts!' I said to myself. 'That would be outrageous.' I was tempted for a minute to take just one doughnut, but fortunately, I was able to convince myself to stick with the rule. 'No, Tam,' I told myself, 'it's three or none.'

"I can't believe what happened next. I walked away without taking any doughnuts, and I went back to my office. It felt really strange, but soon, I could feel myself smiling. I had outfoxed my own addiction! For months, I hadn't been able to keep myself from eating doughnuts. Now, all of a sudden, I was completely turned off by *having* to eat too many of them on purpose. I was right. The strategy is weird. But you were right, too. It works!"

Why does Going Too Far work?

The answer, we believe, will give you another interesting and useful glimpse into the peculiar way the human guidance system is wired.

Tammy first used her smarts to conclude that it was in her best interest to stop eating doughnuts. Then she decided that she would behave in accord with that conclusion—in accord with her mind's intelligent guidance. But because her decision didn't have as much clout as her urge to eat doughnuts did, her decision and her behavior went in opposite directions.

By promising to eat three doughnuts if she ate any at all, Tammy changed everything. She made straying from her intention a much bigger deal. In fact, she made it a big enough deal to convince her Primitive Guidance System to get into the act. Because she now *had* to eat three doughnuts instead of "just one," eating doughnuts was no longer simply a matter of satisfying a craving. Eating doughnuts had become a threat that Tammy could feel. And because she could feel it—not just think it—the PGS was ready and willing to help.

The moral of the story is that while your mixed-up guidance system routinely lets your behavior stray from your intentions, it does have its limits—just like the state trooper on the shoulder of the highway. All you have to do is promise to stray even further than the system normally allows you to, and you'll change everything. By threatening to *purposely* go against your own intelligent guidance, you'll sound the alarm. You'll get the PGS to stop working against your intention and start working for it.

Yvonne used the Going Too Far strategy to cut down on her smoking. "If I smoke a cigarette, I'll smoke a second one immediately after I finish the first one. It's two cigarettes or none at all," she promised.

For weeks before she used the strategy, Yvonne had routinely allowed herself to violate her intention to refrain from smoking. "Now," she explained, "every time I want a cigarette, I think, 'Yuck, I sure don't want to smoke two cigarettes. One is bad enough.' "

Tony used a variation on the Going Too Far strategy to go even further than Yvonne. He quit smoking once and for all.

Tony, who had smoked for over twenty-five years, had been trying to quit for at least the past eight years. He knew in his heart that someday he would have to quit smoking. But when? He logged one failed attempt after another. Yet the window of opportunity on quitting remained open. He knew that if he failed "this time," he could just try quitting again. With the window of opportunity on quitting propped open, Tony continued to smoke.

After learning about Going Too Far, Tony made an interesting deal with himself. "If I don't quit smoking this month, then I won't allow myself to try quitting again for at least a year." In other words, he promised to either finally take advantage of the window of opportunity, or slam it shut and keep it shut for a year.

"I couldn't stand the thought of knowing that if I failed again, I'd *have* to be a smoker for another year," Tony explained. "Even though I'd already smoked for years despite my intention to quit, I was very unsettled by the possibility that I could lose the *opportunity* to quit. It left me with an urgency about quitting that I had never felt before."

So, it was the threat of *having* to violate his intention in a big way that enabled Tony to finally behave in accord with it. Like Tammy and Yvonne, Tony discovered how alarming it can feel—and how energizing it can be—to promise to purposely violate an intention that's already ineffective.

Going Too Far can also prove helpful when you have a strong urge to avoid doing what you intend to do.

For example, if you've been putting off doing paperwork that you really have to get done, you can make a deal like this with yourself: "If I don't work on my paperwork today, I won't work on it tomorrow either."

Marnie used a variation on the Going Too Far strategy to get herself to work on some unpleasant work tasks that she had been avoiding for weeks. Instead of agreeing to purposely postpone working on the tasks if she continued to avoid them, she found another way to kick sand in the face of her intention. She agreed that unless she was working on the dreaded tasks, she would do something to show herself how foolish she was being.

Here's the deal that Marnie made with herself: "If I'm in my office and I'm not working on the tasks when I could be, then I'll stand."

Marnie told us that the deal helped her *feel*—not just *know*—how silly it is to avoid doing things that she'd eventually have to do anyway. "After only a few minutes of standing in my office, I said to myself, 'Marnie, this is ridiculous. Are you going to stand here all day, or are you going to sit down and make a dent in that pile?' I got to work," she told us. "The next time I stood in my office avoiding the tasks, it took me even less time to get to work. Now all I have to do is stand for a second or two and I get the message loudly and clearly."

Just remember, Going Too Far will only work if you're able to honor the deal that you make. If you find that you're not able to keep your promise to cross the line, then this is the wrong strategy for you.

CHAPTER 16

Right Before Wrong

The man who removes a mountain begins by carrying away small stones.

—Anonymous

Abbey was trying to improve her eating habits. "The thing I'm having the most trouble with is between-meals snacks," she said. "I know what I should be eating. I think about eating some carrot sticks or a piece of celery, but when I get to the kitchen, I usually end up reaching for something fattening instead."

We introduced Abbey to a follow through strategy that we call *Right Before Wrong*. Like the Going Too Far strategy, the Right Before Wrong strategy doesn't require you to fight an urge to do the wrong thing. And also like the Going Too Far strategy, it requires you to make a deal—to follow a rule. But with the Right Before Wrong strategy, instead of promising to do more of the wrong thing, you promise to do the right thing *before* you do the wrong thing.

The Right Before Wrong strategy is pretty specialized. It

works only in those situations like Abbey's where you have an urge to do the wrong thing but no real reluctance to do the right thing.

Abbey wasn't reluctant to eat the kind of snack foods she decided she should eat. "I don't mind eating raw vegetables," she told us. "The only reason I don't eat them is because there are lots of other things—unfortunately all more fattening—that I enjoy eating a whole lot more."

We asked Abbey to make a deal with herself. "From now on, when you want a snack, first eat the right foods. Then, after you're done, go ahead and have the wrong foods if you still want them. In other words, have a celery stick. When you're finished eating it, if you still want a piece of chocolate cake, go right ahead."

"Won't I just end up having two snacks instead of one?" she asked.

"Sometimes you will," we replied. "But by eating the right foods first, you'll give yourself a chance to get into the habit of eating the right foods. You may also make yourself less hungry for the wrong foods. And because you're not forbidding yourself to eat the wrong foods if you still want them, you'll avoid the usual tug-of-war that results from trying to deprive yourself of something you want."

Abbey got good results with the Right Before Wrong strategy. Sometimes, but not often, she did go ahead and eat the wrong foods after eating the right ones. But she always ate the right foods. And more often than not, the right foods satisfied her hunger.

Winning a Wrestling Match Without Getting Into the Ring

Marty used the Right Before Wrong strategy to follow through on his intention to watch less TV and read more.

Marty had gotten into the habit of coming home from work, eating supper in front of the TV, and then just camping there for the entire evening. Although, he told us, the habit got started because there was a particular program that he wanted to watch, that program had been canceled months ago and replaced with one he didn't really like. What's more, he didn't care much for most of the other programs he ended up watching every evening.

"It really ticks me off," Marty complained. "There's a lot of good stuff I could be reading instead of just taking in all this dribble from the tube. I keep telling myself to turn off the TV and pick up one of the many books or articles I've been meaning to read for months. But I just keep staring at the crap on TV, all the while hating it and hating myself for doing it."

Fortunately, Marty realized that solving this problem was going to take more than just giving himself another "That's enough, Buster" speech. He was ready to stop spinning his wheels and to start using a follow through strategy.

"Marty," we asked, "do you feel any resistance to reading? In other words, if the TV didn't work, would you read?"

"Hey, I like to read," he replied. "I used to do it all the time in the evenings. I don't think I'm reluctant at all to read. I just think I'm stuck in a bad habit."

"Well, let's see if we can get you out of that habit, not by wrestling with it, but by outfoxing it," we said. "Let's sketch out a plan, okay?"

"You're not going to tell me to break my TV or get rid of it, are you? I've heard about you guys," laughed Marty.

"Let's label that 'Plan B,' " we replied. " 'Plan A' is gentler. Here's what we want you to do: First, choose a book or magazine that you would be reading in the evening if you weren't watching TV. Keep that book or magazine in, or right next to, the chair you sit in to watch TV. After each TV program is over, turn off the TV, pick up the book or magazine, and start reading. If you still want to watch the next program, DON'T fight the urge. Turn the TV back on but keep the sound off until the next program starts. Continue to read while you're waiting for the next show to start. If, by the time the show starts, you're into reading and feel like continuing, you can turn the TV off, but don't hesitate to turn it back on anytime you want. Just make sure that right after each program you watch is over, you turn off the TV and start reading.

"Now, Marty, think carefully before answering: Do you see any possible reason why you wouldn't be able to follow this plan? It's not the right strategy if there's anything at all about it that you know you'll have trouble doing," we said.

"I'm pretty sure I can do it," he replied. "The only concern I have is that I might get irritated with myself if I do want to turn the TV back on instead of continuing to read," he said. "What should I do if that happens?"

"Good question," we answered. "No matter how irritated you get, don't fight the urge to turn the TV back on. Avoiding a power struggle is what makes this strategy work."

"I'm willing to give it a try," Marty said. "It sure sounds better than Plan B."

"It is better than Plan B," we replied. "That's why we suggested it. But if Plan A doesn't work, you'll have to decide which is better: Plan B, or being held hostage by a habit that's wasting your time and making you feel lousy about yourself."

Fortunately for Marty, he didn't have to make that choice. The Right Before Wrong strategy worked. He didn't totally replace watching TV with reading. But he broke his unproductive habit. By turning off the TV and starting to read between TV programs, he often got involved enough in his reading to keep going after the next show started.

"I'm now much more selective about what I watch," Marty told us. "If there's nothing really good on TV, I read. Some evenings now, I watch the news and that's it. I feel like I'm finally in charge of my own evenings. And I know that if I ever start to slide back into my old ways, I can always use the same strategy again.

"Thanks, guys," Marty chuckled, "for helping me solve this problem without taking away my TV set. I have to admit that the thought of having to implement Plan B helped me carry out Plan A!"

"Touché," we replied.

CHAPTER 17

Strike While the Iron Is Hot

He who hesitates is a damned fool.

—Mae West

Katherine, whose dog had wandered off in a blizzard and gotten lost, was thrilled when she got a call from a woman who lived several miles away saying that she had found Katherine's dog. Katherine really appreciated what this woman had done. Not only had she rescued the dog and taken good care of it for a couple of days, she had gone to great lengths to find the dog's owner.

When Katherine went to pick up the dog, she offered the woman a reward. The woman graciously declined. "I'm just glad for both of you that your dog is back where she belongs," the woman said.

Katherine was so grateful, all she could think about on the way home was sending the woman who rescued her dog a gift or at least a nice thank you card. She thought about what kind of gift and what kind of card might be best. The next day, Katherine continued to think about gifts and cards, but she didn't make any final decisions. Ditto the day after, and the day after that. After a few days, Katherine was no longer thinking much about a gift or a card. Once in a while, something would happen—like when the dog wasn't right there when Katherine got home one night, or when she heard about a possible blizzard on the weather report—to remind her of the woman's good deed and of Katherine's own good intention to formally express her appreciation. But Katherine never did get around to doing what she intended to do. What's more, she felt awful about it.

Katherine made a big mistake. It's the same mistake that many of us make. We don't quite realize that when it comes to intentions like Katherine's, we have to strike while the iron is hot because the iron won't stay hot for long. If you don't act on your intention soon, you might as well consider it history—a "regret-in-the-making."

How could Katherine have prevented her regret? If she understood that, because of the way the mind works, her good intention was bound to cool, she could have made a point of taking some kind of action while the iron was still hot. Even if she couldn't decide whether to just send a card or to send a gift too, she could have immediately taken a tangible step in the right direction. She could have, for example, taken a generic card out of the box she had in her desk, addressed an envelope, and then left them on the kitchen counter where she would see them every day. She could then have decided to just send the generic card by Friday unless by then she'd found a better card or thought of a good gift to get. But by leaving the whole matter on her "pending list," Katherine let the iron cool and the intention die. She created a new regret that would live on for years.

The *Strike While the Iron Is Hot* strategy is the perfect

strategy to use whenever you have an intention that was born while your emotions were being "stirred." The strategy acknowledges that inspiration doesn't last long; that when the stirring stops, the window of opportunity for following through begins to shut; that unless you take some kind of action—at least do something to get the ball rolling—while your emotions are still engaged, you'll likely lose the opportunity to follow through.

Evan used the Strike While the Iron Is Hot strategy to follow through on a great idea he picked up at a conference.

"I'm sure I've heard about hundreds of terrific ideas at the seminars, workshops, and classes I've attended in the last ten years. But when I stop and think about how many of those great ideas I've actually put into practice, I realize that I could count them on one hand and still have a couple of fingers left over," Evan confessed.

"It's weird. Even the ideas that excite me the most are usually gone by the time I get home," said Evan. "By *gone,* I don't mean that I actually forget what the ideas were. I remember them, alright. And I still think they're great ideas that I really should implement. The problem is, I no longer feel like implementing them."

Just before going to a conference in Chicago a couple of months ago, Evan had a lunch with a colleague who told Evan all about the Strike While the Iron Is Hot strategy. "Try it at the conference," his friend urged. Evan was intrigued, but made no promises either to his colleague or to himself.

At the conference, every time Evan heard about an idea that sounded good to him, he did the usual. He would simply think, "That's a good idea. I'll start doing it as soon as I get home." But on the second day of the conference, he heard about an especially good idea that had to do with scheduling appointments with clients specifically to get feedback about the service they'd received.

Just as Evan was about to think, "That's a great idea. I'll start doing it as soon as I get home," a very different thought popped into his head. "Who are you kidding, Ev?" he challenged. "Do something now or forget it." He was shocked. But he took the new advice seriously.

Evan waited impatiently for the speaker to finish and then made a beeline for the telephone. He called his secretary, gave her a list of clients, and told her to contact them to schedule appointments over the next several weeks.

Evan struck while the iron was hot. While he was still all fired up about a great idea, he took action to make sure that he would benefit from the idea long after he had cooled down.

"I realize now that making that phone call from the conference was like rushing to the bank to cash a big check signed in disappearing ink!" he explained. "Had I waited, like I used to do, my excitement would have cooled, and I would have ended up getting absolutely nothing out of an idea that, instead, has already helped me bring in thousands of dollars in new business."

To use the Strike While the Iron Is Hot strategy requires very little skill. What it requires most is adjusting your attitude to reflect how the mind really works. All you have to remember is this: "If you intend to do it because you're inspired, either take action now or kiss the intention goodbye."

Pay Now, Buy Later

Anthony, a self-proclaimed cheapskate, figured out how to use his passion for economy to fuel follow through.

"When's the last time you had the oil changed?" barked the mechanic who was examining Anthony's ailing car.

"I'm not exactly sure," said Anthony, knowing that it was much longer ago than it should have been.

Anthony felt embarrassed and stupid. "I can't believe how negligent I am about stuff like this," he scolded himself. "I've got to start taking better care of my car. I definitely can't afford to replace it."

This wasn't the first time Anthony swore he would start taking better care of his car. "I keep promising myself I'll do it, but then I never follow through," he admitted. "The only time I ever get the oil changed is when the car needs repairs."

Just then, Anthony noticed a sign on the wall in the service department waiting room. The sign advertised an oil change card. "Buy it today for just $99," said the sign, "and get up to eight oil changes over the next two years."

"What a perfect plan for me!" Anthony realized. "I'll buy the card now while I'm thinking about how important preventive maintenance is. If I wait, I'll probably forget all about it."

As he paid for the card, Anthony congratulated himself on his smart move. "By paying for the oil changes in advance," he reasoned, "I'll be motivated to get my money's worth. And that means I'll want to get the oil changed often."

Did it work?

You bet it did.

"Hey, I can hardly wait for the odometer to say 'It's time again,' " Anthony told us after his fourth "free" oil change. "My car's never had it this good. And even though it may not be for the right reason, I feel great about finally following through."

CHAPTER 18

Meet the MotivAider®: Your Electronic Follow Through Assistant

---

Better to light a candle than to curse the darkness.

—Chinese Proverb

The MotivAider is the only device we know of that was created explicitly to help people follow through on their good intentions.

Used worldwide in the fields of health care, education, sports, and business, the MotivAider has helped people of all ages achieve a seemingly endless variety of goals.

When I (Pete) came across the MotivAider about five years ago, I was blown away. Behind an unassuming electronic device—it does nothing more than count and shake—stood a powerful realization about human nature and an ingeniously simple way to tackle an age-old problem. Within hours of using the MotivAider for the first time, the device had taught me two lessons that I will never ever forget: (1) Success in all things big and small depends on follow through; and (2) The human mind needs just a little bit of the right kind of help to make it work a whole lot better.

The MotivAider concept emerged from Steve's discovery over fifteen years ago that the mind, amazingly, has no built-in mechanism to keep our attention focused on our good intentions, and that without such a mechanism, intentions are bound to get lost in the shuffle.

Steve conceived of the MotivAider as the intention-supporting mechanism that the human mind is missing. The MotivAider was his answer to the question, "What would you have to add to the human mind to make follow through the rule rather than the exception?" As it turned out, it wasn't necessary to add much at all.

Designing a Follow Through Device

When I (Steve) set out to design a device to enable people to do a better job of following through, I thought about what engineers do when they set out to add a specific capability to a machine. I realized that they usually try to get as much help as possible from what the machine already does. For example, when automotive engineers first set out to figure out a way to keep passengers warm in the winter, they realized that they didn't actually have to produce more heat. There was already plenty of heat available as a by-product of the work the engine was doing. So the engineers concentrated on figuring out a way to capture the heat the engine was already producing and direct it to the car's interior.

I searched for something the human mind already does that I could build on—something about the way it works that could be used to help it do a better job of following through. I eventually found what I was looking for. I discovered a way to improve follow through by capitalizing on how the mind reacts to reminders or cues.

I began with some introspection. I realized that whenever something would happen to remind me of a particular intention, I'd focus my attention on that intention. Whenever the intention was in the spotlight—when it was on "the front burner"—I'd be much more likely to follow through.

I had seen this same phenomenon time and time again with the rehabilitation patients I worked with. As long as they were in the hospital, where they were exposed to lots of cues that reminded them of their intention to do whatever it took to recover quickly and fully, they followed through. But soon after leaving the hospital to return home, where there were fewer cues to remind them of what to do and why to do it, these patients often fizzled out.

I recall talking with Lowell, a farmer who was recovering from an injury to his arm. He did his arm-strengthening exercises faithfully in the hospital. When Lowell was discharged from the hospital, his physician explained how important it would be for Lowell to continue exercising his arm as much as possible. But when he returned a couple of weeks later for an outpatient visit, Lowell confessed that he was doing a lousy job of following through. He was troubled and mystified by his failure. Not only was he eager to regain the strength he'd lost, he didn't even mind doing the prescribed exercises.

"I did great while I was in the hospital," Lowell explained. "I thought about my arm all the time. I thought about how I'd better do the exercises the doctor showed me so I can get my arm back to normal as quickly as possible. But now that I'm home, I just don't think about my arm that much any more. The only time I think about it is when someone asks me how my arm is doing, or when I see someone else with an arm in a cast, or when I go to do something and notice that my arm is still weak. Whenever I think about my arm, I do my exercises. But unless something happens to remind me, I forget all about my arm and all about the exercises."

So whenever Lowell was exposed to the right cues, he behaved in accord with his intention to exercise his arm. Without the right cues to shine a spotlight on his intention, his intention was useless.

I was intrigued. If we humans could count on being exposed to enough of the right cues, the mind would already have what it takes to follow through. I sensed that somehow this insight could be used to create a way for people to follow through on their good intentions. But how?

The "Cue Generator" Concept

Strangely enough, the answer came to me while I was watching a TV documentary on undersea exploration. As I watched a scuba diver descend to the bottom of the ocean, an idea began to rise to the top of my mind. Here's how my thinking went:

Divers want to explore an environment that doesn't provide them with the oxygen they need to breathe. So they've figured out a way to take the oxygen with them. With a scuba tank, divers can thrive in an environment where there's no oxygen available.

Why not do the same thing with cues? We need enough of the right cues to follow through on a good intention. But, like Lowell, we spend most of our time in environments that don't have enough of the right cues available to make and keep our intentions effective. So why not create a "cue tank" or a "cue generator" that people can take with them wherever they go? That way they'd always have enough of the right cues to keep any chosen intention on the front burner.

So I set out to create an "onboard personal cue generator." I called it "The MotivAider."

How the MotivAider Works

The MotivAider is a remarkably simple device. Beeper-like in size and appearance, you carry it in a pocket or clip it to your belt or waistband. It automatically sends you a private signal as often as you choose (as often as once a minute). The signal consists of a gentle, silent vibration that lasts for a couple of seconds.

To use the MotivAider, you first devise a personal message—a word or a short phrase or sentence—that will tune you in to the action you need to take or to a reason that motivates you to take the action. For example, say you've decided that you should stop participating in the incessant whining that's going on at work because it's only making things worse for you and everyone else. From now on, you intend to make sure that your own contribution to conversations is positive and upbeat. Your personal message might simply be, "Upbeat."

After you've decided on a personal message, you decide how often you'd like to receive it. Say you make an educated guess that to follow through on your intention, you'll need to have your attention focused on thinking "Upbeat" at least once every ten minutes.

You simply set the MotivAider for ten minutes and turn it on. The MotivAider is now ready to serve, as one user puts it, "as your intention's full-time guardian angel."

The MotivAider will count down from the ten-minute interval you set, and when it's done counting, the whole device will silently vibrate for a couple of seconds. Then the MotivAider will automatically reset itself to ten minutes, count down again, and vibrate again when it's done counting. It will automatically keep on repeating the cycle of counting down, vibrating, and resetting itself.

So how will all this counting and shaking help you follow

through on your intention to be more positive at work? How can the MotivAider send you your "Upbeat" message? It can't talk, can it?

The MotivAider can't talk. But it doesn't need to talk. Your telephone can't talk, but that doesn't prevent it from sending you the message "Someone is calling" whenever the phone rings. The MotivAider works the same way. You decide what its vibration will mean to you. If it's "Upbeat," then whenever you feel the vibration, the message "Upbeat" will pop into your mind.

If you had a MotivAider at your side automatically focusing your attention on being upbeat at work, here's what you'd experience: Every ten minutes, you'd feel the MotivAider's vibration. Feeling it would automatically make you think the message "Upbeat," which in turn would focus your attention on being positive in conversations. If you began to drift away from your intention, you wouldn't get very far. Soon you'd feel the next vibration, again think "Upbeat," and that would put you right back on track. With a steady stream of private reminders flowing through your mind, urging you to be upbeat, your good intention would have no chance of getting lost in the shuffle.

But what if a gentle tap on the shoulder isn't enough? What if what you really need is a swift kick in the pants? The Motiv-Aider can help. Not only can it remind you of *what* to do, it can remind you of *why* to do it. It can add "motivational muscle" to any intention by keeping you tuned in to an emotionally charged reason for following through on that intention.

For example, suppose you've decided that it's time for you to overcome your reluctance to express your opinion when it differs from the opinions of those around you. Although you want to continue to get along well with people, you've been feeling more and more lately that your lifelong pattern of avoiding disagreement and conflict is doing you more harm than good.

Still, it's not an easy pattern to break, not because you forget what to do, but because you lack the courage to do it.

After doing some soul-searching about what would motivate you to overcome your reluctance to speak up, you realize that one of your biggest fears is that people will view you the way you used to view Bea, a former classmate, who got no respect because she always "agreed" with everyone. All you have to do is think about somebody someday comparing you to Bea, and you can actually feel your intention grow muscles! So you decide to use the MotivAider to keep yourself tuned in to this motivating thought. The message you devise, "To Bea or not to Bea?" should do the trick. With this provocative question popping up in your mind every few minutes, you'll stay motivated to follow through on your intention to express your opinions.

Getting "MotivAided" Without a MotivAider

Although the MotivAider is designed precisely for the purpose of helping people follow through on their intentions, you can benefit from the MotivAider *method* even if you don't have a MotivAider *device*.

First, you'll need to find a signal to use in place of the MotivAider's vibration. There are two requirements for a serviceable signal:

(1) It must reliably get your attention; and
(2) It must occur often enough to serve as a useful cue.

There are two basic sources of signals. One source is from any device that's designed to produce signals. Examples of such devices include alarm watches, electronic organizers and computer programs that have reminder capabilities, oven timers, and alarm clocks. The second source of signals is from sights, sounds, and events that occur around you. Examples are the sound of a phone ringing in a neighboring office, of an airplane passing over, or a circulating fan that makes a noticeable sound whenever it starts or stops, announcements over the PA system, or even the sight of a certain person.

Once you've selected a signal, just follow the same steps you would take if you were using a MotivAider. Devise a message that will tune you into a particular "voice in your crowd" that will make your intention effective. Then, mentally assign the message to the signal so that whenever you receive the signal, it will automatically send you your message.

Dianna found an interesting signal to use as a cue to relax her tense shoulders. She lived in an old house with a hot water heating system that made a clunking noise whenever the furnace operated. She told herself that whenever she heard the clunking sound it would mean to her, "Relax your shoulders."

"It worked great," she said. "The colder it got outside, the more relaxed I was!"

A "Swiss Army Knife" for Your Good Intentions

The MotivAider is a remarkably versatile follow through assistant. It can help you follow through on virtually any intention you choose. By automatically focusing your attention on a chosen intention, the MotivAider enables that intention to have the biggest possible say in how you behave.

Here's a list of actual goals that users have achieved with the MotivAider.

I. At work

- Stay focused at meetings
- Catch others doing things right and praise them

- Adopt a learning or quality improvement mindset
- Use persuasive selling techniques
- Make "cold" calls
- By announcers to breathe properly, use correct posture and intonation
- Keep on moving
- Monitor work activities and refocus whenever necessary on the most important tasks
- Apply learning from workshops and seminars
- Think creatively
- Take periodic relaxation breaks
- Improve presentation skills
- Be a better team player
- Maintain a "follow through mindset"

II. At play

- Improve a golf swing
- Improve a tennis backhand
- Improve bowling technique
- Mentally rehearse basketball free throws
- Refrain from setting the hook prematurely when fishing
- Improve concentration during athletic competition
- Use proper breathing technique when singing

III. Improving health, safety, and fitness

- By persons with cerebral palsy to swallow regularly to prevent drooling
- Improve gait
- Facilitate healing by refraining from using an injured body part
- Use mental imagery to promote healing/recovery
- Drink more water or other fluids
- By diabetics to eat on schedule

- Accept limitations as a way to increase (rather than decrease) freedom
- Practice pain reduction methods
- Carry out bladder training
- Reduce teeth-grinding and jaw-clenching to prevent dental problems and relieve symptoms of TMJ dysfunction
- Follow through on prescribed self-care
- Do Kegel exercises
- Stick with a fitness program
- Stick with a diet
- Eat slowly
- Order the right foods in restaurants
- Quit smoking
- Improve posture
- Keep head up
- Keep back straight
- Practice vision-improvement exercises
- Use proper bending and lifting techniques to prevent back injury
- Drive defensively
- Relax shoulder muscles to prevent muscle tension following a neck injury
- Perform relaxation exercises before and during childbirth

IV. Reducing stress, eliminating unwanted habits, and boosting self-esteem

- Reduce public speaking anxiety
- Breathe deeply
- Monitor and control mood
- Combat negativity
- Fight procrastination
- Stop swearing
- Quit biting fingernails
- Promote restful sleep

- Stay calm during tests
- Implement therapy "homework"
- Think of accomplishments, positive qualities
- Try out a new attitude or outlook or maintain one
- Make specific self-affirmations regularly
- Stay tuned to personal priorities

V. Improving personal image and increasing interpersonal effectiveness

- Act friendlier
- Make frequent eye contact
- Smile more
- Be a better listener
- Avoid getting into unnecessary arguments
- Eliminate unwanted mannerisms
- By parents to look for opportunities to praise their kids
- Act more assertively
- "Try out" new interpersonal behaviors

VI. Personal and spiritual growth

- Enhance creativity, openness
- Stay centered
- Remain in the present
- Carry out mindfulness training
- Practice meditation
- Expand awareness
- Anchor positive emotions
- Induce lucid dreams
- Focus on a spiritual belief or experience
- Think about God regularly

VII. *By teachers*

- Remember to use praise when they feel like yelling
- Effectively monitor students' behavior
- Remember to pay attention to an easily overlooked student
- Apply newly learned techniques or behave in accord with accepted principles

VIII. *By kids*

- On task—to keep their attention from wandering
- Remember to go to the bathroom to prevent bladder and bowel accidents in school
- Interact more effectively with other kids
- Correct speech problems
- Remember to carry out assignments
- Improve self-esteem by remembering accomplishments and abilities
- Eliminate bad habits like thumb-sucking and nail-biting

The MotivAider is manufactured and marketed by Behavioral Dynamics, Inc., P.O. Box 66, Thief River Falls, MN, 56701. (800) 356-1506.

CHAPTER 19

Mary's Follow Through Angel

You can't build a reputation on what you intend to do.

—Liz Smith

Mary was three-quarters of the way through *Following Through*. As she put the book down for the night, she thought to herself, "These strategies sound really neat. I can't wait to try them." Still, she was realistic. She knew that her old ways of treating her intentions wouldn't magically go away. She had grown up with them. They were a part of her. Even though she could now see clearly why they were all wrong, she was rightly prepared for a struggle. "Old habits and old ways of thinking don't die easily," she reminded herself as she went off to sleep.

When she woke up the next morning, Mary was greeted by a surprise. There before her stood a Follow Through Angel.

"I was sent here by Steve and Pete to help you follow through on your good intentions," said the angel. "They warned me not to just perform a few flashy follow through miracles and then leave. My assignment is to help you apply what you've learned about following through so that you can perform your own miracles every day from now on."

Mary, of course, was delighted to have help. And it wasn't very long before she needed it.

When she got to work that morning, Mary was greeted by an angry message from the Purchasing Department. As she read it out loud to the Follow Through Angel, Mary shook her head and said, "This wouldn't have happened if I'd done what I keep promising to do. I can't tell you how many times I've told myself that I have to make a point of talking to the folks in Purchasing every day. All it would take is five minutes a day to prevent communication messes like this one from happening. There's absolutely no good reason why I keep failing to do what I know I should do. I'm so disgusted with myself."

"Whoa, Mary," said the Follow Through Angel. "Do you remember what causes poor follow through?"

"Sure I do. It's caused by the mixed-up way the mind is designed," said Mary. "And if I want to follow through, I have to recognize the design problems and work around them, right?"

"Absolutely," replied the Angel. "You have to stop assuming that having an intention is all it takes to follow through. You can't expect to follow through on your intention to visit Purchasing unless you have a specific plan for following through."

"Well, then, I'll devise a plan right now," said Mary. "First I have to figure out what's keeping me from following through, right? I really don't mind visiting Purchasing at all. In fact, I usually enjoy it—that is, when I remember to do it."

"Bingo!" exclaimed the Angel. "*Remember* is the key word here. There's nothing that happens often enough to remind you to visit Purchasing. There are things that remind you to do nearly everything else you do here. But other than the reminders like that incident report that come too late, what reminds you to visit Purchasing? If you're leaving it up to your mind alone, it's no wonder it's not happening."

"Okay, I need to make sure that something will remind me to do what I intend to do," said Mary. "I have an idea. I have a scheduling program on my computer. I use it to remind myself of meetings. It works great. I never miss a meeting. What if I considered my five-minute daily visit to Purchasing to be a meeting? I'll just put it in my schedule every day. Then the computer will beep and flash to let me know I should go to Purchasing."

"That sounds good," said the Angel. "Frankly, we angels don't know much about computers. But if you can set that program so that it beeps and flashes periodically throughout the day and won't stop until you visit Purchasing, that would be perfect."

"Done," said Mary as she finished entering the right commands. "You know, I'm embarrassed at how long I've been struggling with this Purchasing thing. Yet all it took is a few minutes to set up a plan to solve the problem. Now that I'm on a roll, can you help me with something else? I'm about ten or fifteen pounds overweight. I'd certainly prefer to be thinner. Now that I know how to follow through, I think I'll start a diet today."

"Hold your horses, Mary," said the Angel. "Don't be too quick to make any promises to yourself about dieting. Promising to stick to a diet is a big commitment. Are you sure you're ready? Why not give yourself some time to carefully think through what you'll have to give up and put up with to stay on a diet? Ask yourself if the benefits of losing the weight are worth the trouble. Only make a promise to yourself if you're pretty sure that the answer is Yes."

"Okay then, maybe I'd better think about the whole thing for a while before I make any big decisions," said Mary. "I realize that I've been pretty quick in the past to make promises I can't really keep. I see now that if I'm careless in making a promise, not only is there a good chance that I'll fail, I'll weaken all my future promises in the process."

"That's right," said the Angel. "But perhaps there's a smaller, safer promise that you can make about eating while you're deciding whether to make a much bigger one. Can you think of a specific troublesome eating habit that you can devise a plan to attack?"

"Yeah, I can," Mary replied. "There's a great buffet restaurant around the corner. I go there for lunch two or three times a week. Every time I go there, I give myself a speech about eating moderately. And every time, I end up pigging out. Maybe I can do something to make sure I eat less."

"You sure can. You can promise to stay out of that restaurant in the first place," said the Angel. "If you go there, you're relying far too much on willpower to keep yourself on track. Remember 'leverage'? You're much better off relying on the *situation* to keep you on track. It'll be easier for you to keep a promise to stay out of the restaurant than to keep a promise to eat moderately once you're already there."

"I see your point. But you know, I don't want to go overboard. I know in the past I've often gone too far in restricting myself, and that seems to always backfire. What if I make a commitment to go to the buffet restaurant no more than once a week? I just think that if I close the door completely, I might rebel and end up accomplishing nothing at all."

"That sounds like good thinking and a good plan," replied the Angel. "It always makes sense to use what you've learned about yourself. If you've noticed that whenever you get carried away with setting restrictions, you blow it, then try backing off a little and see what happens. Following through takes a lot of experimenting."

"Speaking of experiments," said Mary, "I sure haven't had much luck with the experiments I've done to try to get my monthly sales reports in on time. I'm afraid I'm going to get myself in big trouble some day if I don't get this problem licked. Any ideas?"

"What happens when you don't get the reports in on time?" asked the Angel.

"Nothing," replied Mary.

"Well, no wonder you're not getting them done," the Angel said. "I assume they're no fun to do, right? So why would you *want* to do them? You'll get them done on time only if you *have* to get them done on time."

"But I know it's important to get the reports done. And I know that I could get in trouble if my boss ever decides to hold me accountable for doing exactly what I'm supposed to do. I always think that these should be good enough reasons to get myself in gear to get the reports done on time, but they're obviously not."

"Remember, Mary, there's a big difference between *good* reasons and *compelling* reasons," the Angel said. "You have *good* reasons to get your reports done on time. But you don't have *compelling* reasons. You need to create a compelling reason."

"Yes, I remember all about compelling reasons now," Mary said as she started to apply what she remembered to the problem at hand. "I know what I can do. How about this? All department heads here have to submit what's called a 'BCD' report monthly. BCD stands for 'Beyond the call of duty.' The purpose of the BCD report is to show the company any creative 'go the extra mile' type of things we're doing to improve performance. I always get these reports in on time because I do a lot of extra stuff that I'm very proud of, and I want the company to know about it. I often get notes back from my boss about how impressed she is by something I reported. What if I decided that from now on I can only submit my BCD report after the monthly sales report is ready to go? I know it would drive me crazy to have to wait to send in the BCD report. I think that would put some friendly pressure on me to get the sales reports done on time."

"That's a great idea," exclaimed the Angel. "I suggest that you add just one thing to it, though. Come up with a heavy-duty backup plan just in case you don't honor the deal you've made with yourself. If you ever submit the BCD report without first submitting the sales report, then it's time to put the heavy-duty plan in motion."

"Okay, I can do that. I remember in the book an example of someone who was going to send a memo to her boss promising to get something done on time from now on. The idea was that by making the promise and putting it in writing, she made following through feel more necessary. I can do the same thing. I'll write an 'I promise' memo now and keep it in my desk. I'll also write in my appointment book right now a note at the end of each month to send the memo unless I've sent my sales report along with or before the BCD report."

"Nice going, Mary!" said the Angel. "You just killed a few birds with one stone. You're really getting the hang of this."

Mary made the entries in her appointment book and was just finishing typing up the "I promise" memo to her boss when a flashing message came up on the computer screen.

"What's that beeping?" the Angel asked.

"It's my reminder to visit Purchasing," replied Mary. "I might as well just do it now."

On her way to the Purchasing Department, Mary greeted Lyle. "Lyle, thanks again for helping me out last week. I really appreciate it. You were a lifesaver."

"What was that all about?" asked the Angel.

"Lyle is an absolute gem. I was having trouble getting my figures squared away on a big proposal that was already a couple of days late. I was tearing my hair out. I asked Lyle if he had a few minutes to help. He ended up spending about an hour and a half with me after work. He not only solved the problem, he helped me improve the proposal, plus I learned some new accounting tricks. And he was so patient with me. Which reminds me, I was going to write a nice thank-you letter to him with a copy to his supervisor. I'm glad I just remembered. I'll have to do that sometime this week."

"Make a U-turn, Mary. Right now!" the Angel said sternly.

"What for?" Mary asked.

"You're thinking right now about your intention to write Lyle a thank-you letter," the Angel answered. "What makes you think you'll think about it again soon enough to do something about it? This intention will never be stronger than it is right now. It already got lost in the shuffle once. Don't let it happen again. If you don't do something about it now, you're pretty much 'deciding' that you won't ever do anything about it. So if you're serious about writing the letter, go do something about it right now. If this isn't a good time to write the letter, at least take some kind of action now that will increase the chances that you'll write the letter when you can."

"I remember," responded Mary. " 'Strike while the iron is hot,' right? I can't tell you how many intentions I've lost before by not striking while the iron is hot. And I still feel badly about every one of them. I'll go back to my office right now, open a file on my computer, and type in 'Dear Lyle' so it will be there when I get back later and can work on it. I'll also write 'Letter to Lyle?' in my appointment book for this Friday to make sure that I've done it. How's that?"

"Terrific!" said the Angel.

"Aren't you coming with me?" asked Mary as she headed back to her office.

"Nope," said the Angel, smiling. "My work here is done."

"Thanks," said Mary. "But aren't you going to at least wish me luck?"

"Nope," replied the Follow Through Angel as she readied her wings for the long trip home. "Luck is what you need when you don't know how to follow through. You don't need luck any more."

How Well Do the Follow Through Experts Follow Through?

The truth is, we're much better at following through than we used to be—particularly when it comes to the things that matter the most. We've definitely become much more cautious about taking on intentions in the first place. We usually catch ourselves before reflexively saying, "I will." And when we do carefully consider an intention and decide to adopt it, we almost always take our commitment *very* seriously.

Still, we'd be less than honest if we left you with the impression that we've managed to completely plug that black hole in inner space where good intentions disappear. Although we have far fewer and far less consequential follow through failures than ever before, we still do have our share of failures. Every now and then we "swing at a bad pitch." An intention with an especially pretty face comes along, and suddenly we forget everything we've learned and everything we teach.

We're confident that we know how to compensate for the mixed-up way the mind treats good intentions. Still, we have no illusions that we'll ever be able to completely make up for the fact that the mind is so poorly designed for follow through. We fully expect our follow through batting averages to continue to improve. But we don't expect to ever bat a thousand.

CHAPTER 20

Using Your Follow Through Toolkit

The hardest thing to learn in life is which bridge to cross and which to burn.

—David Russell

Okay, let's get specific. Let's see how you can use your follow through toolkit to help you follow through on four common intentions:

(1) Sticking to a diet or quitting smoking
(2) Changing a negative attitude
(3) Achieving your financial goals
(4) Improving your relationships

Remember, the key to successfully following through on any intention is to get your Primitive Guidance System (PGS) to cooperate with your Intelligence-Based Guidance System. Each follow through strategy has its own particular way of getting your PGS to stop interfering with follow through and to start helping instead.

First, let's briefly review the strategies.

Spotlighting lets you stay tuned in to the right "voices in your crowd"—the ones that make you feel like acting in accord with your intention.

Willpower Leveraging allows you to get the biggest bang out of every buck of willpower you have. It lets you use a small amount of willpower now to dramatically reduce the amount of willpower you'll need later on to follow through.

Creating Compelling Reasons gets your PGS pushing hard in the right direction. It gives your PGS a reason to use its raw power to propel an intention to victory.

Leading the Horse to Water lets you conquer the problem of avoidance by separating the easy part of an intention from the hard part. By requiring you to do only the easy part, this strategy allows you to build the momentum you need to do the hard part.

Going Too Far and *Right Before Wrong* are helpful when the PGS is pushing you hard to do the wrong thing. By requiring you to violate your intention in a big way if you violate it at all, Going Too Far makes poor follow through a problem that even your PGS will want to solve. Right Before Wrong, by requiring you only to do the right thing before you do the wrong thing, allows you to avoid the kind of power struggle that your intention would surely lose.

Strike While the Iron Is Hot lets you benefit from a fleeting intention before the inspiration that made it possible fades.

Stick to a Diet or Quit Smoking:

- You can accomplish a lot by making a promise to the right person in the right way. You can leverage your will-power and give yourself a compelling reason to follow through by putting yourself on the hook with someone who you'd either hate to disappoint or love to please. Be sure to make your promise in whatever form it takes to make you *feel*—not just *be*—accountable. Make it in writing, in front of a group, in the newspaper—in skywriting, if that's what it takes.

- Don't be afraid to "turn up the heat." Pressure can be your friend rather than your enemy. Give someone a hammer to hold over your head and the authority to use it if you don't follow through. For example, write out a check to an organization you absolutely hate and give it to a friend who agrees to mail the check unless you follow through.

- The right person can be a bountiful source of helpful cues. Share your intention with people who are likely to ask you often about your progress. Or get a coach or join a program that includes a personal coach who will have a stake in your success and who is motivated to see to it that you follow through.

- Leverage your willpower wherever possible. Avoid temptation if you can, but if you are tempted to do the wrong thing, make it as difficult as possible to actually do it. For example, cross the street before you pass the bakery or convenience store; leave your money in your office before you walk by the candy or cigarette vending machine; ask your spouse to stop bringing home those chips you love; clear the house of ashtrays, matches, and lighters; call ahead to order the right foods (before you're tempted by the wrong ones on the menu), or eat somewhere where smoking is prohibited; write a letter to a local charity promising to donate all the edible holiday gifts you receive this year, or promise to donate the money you save by not buying cigarettes.

- Never overlook the power of situations to influence your behavior. Seek out situations in which you typically do the right thing. For example, go to lunch with people who make you feel like eating right, or socialize with people who won't tolerate smoking; plan your evening around an activity or schedule that's been associated before with good eating habits or not smoking.

- Do everything you can to keep your intention in the spotlight. Place reminders of what you want to accomplish and why (or of what you're afraid will happen if you don't follow through) wherever you'll stumble across them. Or use the MotivAider or another alerting device to automatically fill your mind every ten minutes with an image that reminds you of why it's worth the trouble to follow through.

- Energize your intention by threatening to violate it in a big way. Make a deal with yourself that you'll have two ice cream sundaes if you have one, or smoke two cigarettes (one right after the other) if you smoke one. Or require yourself to eat the right foods before eating the wrong foods or to chew a stick of gum or try a relaxation technique before smoking a cigarette.

Changing a Negative Attitude:

- The key to changing your attitude or outlook is to keep your intention in the spotlight. Look for ways to make sure that you'll stay tuned both to *what* to do and *why* to do it.

- Write reminders on your calendar, place notes in your pockets, purse, or wallet, or sprinkle them throughout the pile of papers on your desk.

- Create your own cues out of frequent, naturally occurring events—like the phone ringing, the sound of voices in the hall outside your office or of an airplane passing overhead, or the weird noise your broken refrigerator makes whenever the compressor starts.

- Put a coin or a key in your shoe for the day and use the sensation you get when you step on it as a cue for adopting the right attitude. Or put an unusual object in your pocket that will serve as a cue whenever you feel it.

- Find a photo, a news clip, a rock, or even an old sock that for you symbolizes the change you want to make and an inspiring reason to make it. Place it somewhere where you can't help but notice it often. Use a MotivAider, an alarm watch, another alerting device, or a computer screen-saver or other computer program to send yourself frequent reminders to check and correct your attitude.

- Remember, people can be wonderful cues. Identify people who will take an interest in your progress and turn them into cues by letting them in on your intention.

- Capitalize on your own observations about how people and situations affect your attitude. Spend as much time as possible in the company of people who seem to stimulate the right attitude. That could take the form of joining a club, taking a class, or volunteering for a special project. And do your best to stay away from people and situations that you know from experience only stimulate the wrong attitude.

- Inspiring books and tapes can help, but only if you keep rereading and relistening. And remember, you don't have to reread an entire book or relisten to an entire tape to get reinspired. The right paragraph or page, or the right couple of minutes of a tape, may be all it takes.

Achieving Your Financial Goals:

Saving or Investing:

- Take advantage of automatic savings and investment plans offered by banks, mutual funds, and employers. These plans not only make good financial sense, they make good follow through sense. They allow you to get lots of bang out of every buck of effort you invest in getting started.

- If an automatic savings or investment plan is out of the question, then decide now on the dates you're going to make deposits and write them now on your calendar.

- If you've been putting off a saving or investment plan because you can't decide how much to save or invest, remove resistance by starting now with the smallest allowable contribution. Or energize your intention by kicking sand in its face—agree that unless you start a plan by the beginning of next month, you'll put it off for at least another six months.

- If you intend to invest but keep putting it off, set a deadline, write out a check now for an investment you think is stupid, and give the check to a friend to mail unless you replace it with a wiser choice before a deadline.

- Take steps to keep your financial objectives in the spotlight. Get involved with other people who are interested in improving their financial condition. Consider joining an investment club or taking a class; subscribing to a financial newsletter or magazine; getting yourself on a mailing list for investment publications and products; or listening to a financial management program on TV or radio.

- Schedule a "weekly money management review" with your spouse or partner. Remove a major obstacle to following through by requiring yourself to do nothing more than get a beverage, gather together the materials you need for the review, and sit down at the table for five minutes.

- Stimulate follow through by creating vivid continuous demonstrations of how following through is paying off. For example, use a simple chart, a pile of shoe boxes, or a jar of pennies to show how your savings are accumulating or how your debt is shrinking. If there's a particular goal you're striving for, like saving enough money to buy a new car, then use a picture or a key to symbolize what you're aiming for. Be creative. Design a simple but compelling display that makes your progress unmistakable.

- Find something special that you and your family can do or buy (like go to Disney World or get a Ping-Pong table) when you achieve each financial milestone along the path you've charted. If you have kids, don't forget to get them involved. Kids can be great cheerleaders—great sources of cues. They won't allow your good intentions to get lost in the shuffle.

- Making the right promise to the right person in the right way always helps. For example, identify someone who you'd love to impress with your follow through or who you'd hate to have see you as a quitter. Then promise that person in writing that you'll be saving or investing regularly, and encourage him or her to ask you periodically for progress reports.

Controlling Spending:

There are two keys to curbing your spending: (1) Changing the situation to make it harder to do the wrong thing. (2) Using cues to keep you tuned in to a motivating reason to follow through.

- If you don't intend to spend, then whenever possible, avoid situations that stimulate your desire to buy. If you can't avoid temptation, then do everything you can to limit your opportunity to buy. For example, close charge accounts you don't intend to use; leave your credit cards at home if possible; take only as many blank checks as you intend to use (write "For Emergency Only" in the memo section of any extra checks).

- When you can't restrict your opportunity to spend, then do whatever you can to make it psychologically harder to spend. For example, let your partner know what your intended spending limit is before you go shopping.
- Keep your reasons for not spending in the spotlight. Keep your credit card in a little envelope that has an important personal financial goal written on it. Or keep a rubber band around your card or checkbook as a reminder of your goals. Or decide that a certain watch, bracelet, or special pair of shoes you own will stand for an important financial goal, and wear that item on days when you know that the temptation will be the greatest.
- If, and only if, you're able to follow some simple rules, you can make it harder to buy stuff that you don't intend to buy and still avoid a power struggle. For example, instead of saying "No way" to an item you want badly to buy but shouldn't, say "Hold off (and go elsewhere) for at least thirty minutes." Or require yourself to go too far, that is, to deliberately buy a particular item you know is really stupid if you "accidentally" buy something that you shouldn't. Or require yourself to say or do something embarrassing (like telling a sales clerk that you've given up on your financial future, or kissing your money goodbye in the store) before you make an unintended purchase. Or require yourself to do the right thing before doing the wrong thing, for instance, by allowing only those items that you intended to buy in your cart and going all the way to the checkout line before permitting yourself to go back for anything else.

Improving Your Relationships:

- Make it easy to start doing the right thing in the relationships you want to improve. Instead of insisting on hitting a grand slam right away, settle for making it to the ball-park. For example, if you intend to become *much* more involved in your son's or daughter's life, then agree only to become ever-so-slightly more involved. Start now by promising yourself that you'll devote your undivided attention to your daughter for ten minutes on Thursday nights when you're home. Try this same approach if you intend to be more attentive to your partner's needs.

- If you're not following through for the right reasons, instead of giving up, try following through for the wrong reasons. For example, tell your golfing foursome—and your spouse—that unless you spend time playing with your kids twice this week, you won't be playing golf on Saturday. Or promise your kids that unless you come home from work on time, they can watch a particular TV program that you'd really rather they not see. Or use leverage to lock yourself in to spending time with your child by volunteering now to help out with an activity that your child is involved in.

- Relationship-improvement intentions are among the first to get lost in the shuffle. Keep yourself tuned in to your intentions by, for example, keeping a book or article about parenting or marriage on your nightstand or desk to remind you of your intention. (Who knows, someday you might even read it!)

- Use an alerting device to keep yourself tuned in to the particular "voices in your crowd" that know that it's more important, for example, to get along with somebody you love than it is to be right; to listen more and talk less; or to bolster rather than undermine a loved one's self-confidence. Or use it to remind yourself to be attentive to a partner's or coworker's needs, or to keep yourself tuned in to a child-rearing principle or technique that you *preach* but forget to *practice*.

- Don't hesitate to stimulate a weak intention by kicking sand in its face. For example, if you intend to be a better listener, make a deal with yourself that if you don't do a good job of listening, you'll deliberately interrupt the next person you talk to. Or agree that if you violate your intention to stop being excessively critical of your wife, you'll deliberately go even further than usual and blame her for everything, including the rotten weather.

The Follow Through Mindset

If we are to achieve results never before accomplished, we must expect to employ methods never before attempted.

—Francis Bacon

The Follow Through Mindset: An Overview

To follow through consistently, you need more than follow through strategies. You need to make some fundamental changes in the way you understand and treat your own intentions.

The purpose of this section is to help you adopt what we call a "Follow Through Mindset." It's a new perspective—a new model—for understanding and treating your own intentions. It's a model that's based not on fairy tale notions of how the mind *should* work, but on the truth about how it really *does* work.

Of course, it would be a whole lot easier for you to adopt the new model if you didn't already have a model in place. But you do. And although the old model doesn't work, it's built as solid as a rock. Not only have you grown up with it, it's been extremely well-maintained by the culture in which you live.

So, unfortunately, before you start installing the new model, you have some demolition work to do. You have to identify and tear down the old model. A warning: This won't be easy. Much of the old model sits "underground." Its assumptions are so deeply ingrained in your thinking that they're nearly invisible. And not only are they hard to spot, they're hard to remove permanently. Like weeds, they'll grow back if you give them a chance.

CHAPTER 21

Adopting Intentions Is Serious Business

I was put on the earth to accomplish a certain number of things. Right now, I'm so far behind, I'll never die!
—Anonymous

They call it "overbooking." The airlines do it all the time. In their desire to sell as many seats as they can, the airlines do their best to sell *more* seats than they have. They do it because they know that some passengers who make reservations won't show up.

Of course, Mother Nature does it too. In fact, you could say that she invented overbooking. Female lobsters, for example, lay up to 100,000 eggs as a hedge against all the things that can go wrong. Apparently lots of things *do* go wrong. Out of 100,000 eggs, only four lobsters will reach maturity.

If you look at how many good intentions we humans produce, and how many of them never "hatch," it's tempting to conclude that overbooking is the way we humans make sure that at least *some* of our intentions will make it.

Nothing could be further from the truth. Overbooking isn't the reason some of our intentions survive. Overbooking, or at least careless booking, is the reason so many of our intentions die young.

There's one thing we learned for sure as a result of our study of follow through over the past few years: We humans *break* too many promises because we *make* too many promises.

We treat our intentions as if they were a dime a dozen.

It takes precious little for us to turn a "Hey, that sounds like a good idea," into a "Yes, I intend to do that." Instead of carefully checking out a prospective intention the way we'd check out a prospective marriage partner or a prospective new home, a prospective new job, or even a prospective new pair of shoes, we just jump right in and, bingo, we make a promise. It's easy. We rarely pause long enough to realize that the easier it is to make a promise, the easier it is to break it too.

But making careless promises is not our only mistake. We also make too many of them. We're like the assembly line worker who, when confronted with the fact that he had misassembled every single widget he made that day, responded with, "Well yeah, I can see that they're no good. But don't I at least get credit for making so many of them?"

We treat our intentions the way negligent parents treat their children. We let them come and go as they please.

We freely take on new intentions even though the "ship" is so overcrowded with old intentions that they're falling overboard. "Hey, no big deal," we figure. "There are plenty more where those came from."

We grossly underestimate the cost of failing to follow through on any given intention. We assume that all we stand to lose are the direct benefits of behaving in accord with that intention; that, for example, if you don't follow through on your intention to keep your desk clean, all you'll miss out on are the benefits of having a clean desk. But we're wrong. We stand to lose a lot more.

You see, every time you fail to take an intention seriously, you reduce the power and influence of all your intentions.

We know Frank Lee Clueless would disagree. "C'mon, guys, lighten up!" he'd shout. "What's the big deal? No one else has to know about the promises I make to myself. So what if I don't keep them? What difference can it possibly make?"

Well, Frank, from what we can tell, failing to keep a promise you make to yourself has the same effect as failing to keep a promise you make to someone else.

Suppose you promise Mary that by Thursday you'll return the book you borrowed from her. And suppose you don't make good on your promise. What will happen the next time you ask her if you can borrow a book? Chances are, you'll have less credibility the second time around. What if Mary reluctantly gives you another chance and you screw up again? How believable do you suppose your third promise will be? How about your fourth one? What if you ask to borrow her lawn mower "for just a couple of days?"

Break a promise you make to yourself—that is, adopt an intention and then fail to behave in accord with it—and your next intention will have less clout. *Make a habit* of adopting intentions and then failing to behave in accord with them, and you'll end up with intentions that, like comedian Rodney Dangerfield, "Don't get no respect."

A Promise Is a Promise

If you want to make sure that all your intentions start out with maximum clout, then repeat after us: "Adopting intentions is serious business."

Just because you've produced an intention doesn't mean you should adopt it. If you want the intentions you adopt to be as credible, powerful, and influential as possible, you've got to start being more selective.

Never adopt an intention without realizing that you're making a serious commitment. Think about it this way: When you adopt an intention, you're making a promise, giving your word, putting your reputation and your credibility on the line. Don't do it unless you're confident that you really know what it will take to keep that promise. Don't do it unless you're ready, able, and willing to actually do what it takes.

If you take an intention any less seriously than that, you'll not only cheapen that particular intention, you'll cheapen them all. If you treat your intentions as if they're a dime a dozen, that's about what they'll be worth.

Date Before You Marry

There's a model you can use for knowing how much care to take in deciding whether to adopt an intention that will require you to make a difficult and sustained change. Just think about the intention as if it were a prospective mate.

No matter how strong the initial attraction may be, few of us actually make a long-term commitment to a prospective mate within minutes of meeting that person. It's not very often that "love at first sight" results in an instant marriage proposal. People do get swept off their feet. But even the ones who fall the hardest usually exercise some restraint. And for most of us, initial attraction, rather than triggering a commitment, triggers a decision to get to know a prospective mate better. We decide, in other words, to *date* before we marry.

When we date, we look for compatibilities and incompatibilities. We see how a prospective mate "wears" over time. And only if things go "well enough for long enough," do we consider making a commitment.

Even if it sweeps you off your feet, "date" a new intention

before deciding to "marry" it. Hold off on making any promises until you've had a chance to get to know the intention well enough to have some idea of what it would really be like to be married to it. Take some time to see how much it will cost you to behave in accord with the intention. And take enough time to get a feel for whether the benefits of following through will actually be worth the trouble.

If you think it would be a good idea, for example, to begin an exercise program, don't make any promises to yourself right away. First spend some time "flirting" with the idea. By all means, do some exercising if the spirit moves you. But hold off on making any firm commitments until you have a pretty good idea of what life would be like—both for better and for worse—if you were to actually go ahead and take the plunge.

Preventing Mistakes

If you're wondering if the cautiousness we're preaching could discourage you from adopting some pretty important intentions, all we can say is, "We certainly hope so."

The fact is, dating your intentions before marrying them will prevent some important intentions from ever reaching the altar. But this is good news, not bad news. When you consider how much you stand to lose if an intention fails, it's hardly a tragedy to prevent a "bad marriage" from happening in the first place.

Have a Ceremony

Suppose you've concluded that a particular intention is right for you? How do you actually go about adopting it?

The short answer is, do what most people do when they get married: Have a ceremony!

The idea of having a ceremony to make a commitment feel more serious and real is deeply rooted in our culture.

Exactly what an intention-adoption ceremony should consist of is entirely up to you. But it should, at the very minimum, include making some kind of formal record of your decision to adopt the intention.

Janice not only had a ceremony, she had a whole system for making her promises feel real. She kept a jar with a label on it that said "Promise Bank" on her kitchen counter. In the jar were index cards—each a record of a particular intention she had adopted. Next to the jar, she kept a few blank "Promise Cards" that she made on her home computer. Here's what Janice printed on each of the cards:

"On_____, after careful consideration, I've decided to make a commitment to_____."

Whenever Janice decided to adopt an intention, she would take a Promise Card and fill in the date and a brief description of what she intended to do. Then she would slowly read the Promise Card out loud twice, give herself one last chance to throw the card away (something she actually did on three occasions), deposit the card in the jar, and replace the lid.

Janice told us that her intention-adoption ceremony had gradually evolved to include an out-loud review of *all* the Promise Cards in the jar. "It helps me stay on top of the promises I've made to myself," she said. "I can see all the commitments I've made in a tangible form. And when there are too many cards in the jar, I get especially careful about making new promises," said Janice.

Breaking Up Is Hard To Do

Suppose an intention makes it through the dating process with flying colors. You feel it's right for you. So you go ahead and adopt it. You even have a ceremony to underscore your commitment. Everything goes along fine for a while. But then trouble starts to brew. It gets harder and harder to behave in accord with the intention. Not that you expected it to be easy, but somehow you thought you'd feel that the effort was a whole lot more worthwhile than it's actually been feeling. It's clear to you that had you known before what you know now, you wouldn't have decided to adopt this intention.

What can you do?

Well, here's what most of us do: We let the intention die a quiet death. We kill it with neglect. We allow our behavior to stray further and further from the intention until the intention is history.

This is positively the worst way to deal with an intention that you've grown weary of.

Our advice: No matter how convinced you are that an intention is no longer right for you, never, ever let it fade away! Treating any intention that way will only rob all your intentions of influence.

Does that mean that you're stuck for life with an intention that you no longer believe in?

Fortunately, the answer is No. There's a way to get out of a bad "marriage" without undermining the influence of your other intentions. The right way is, you guessed it, to "divorce," the intention. That's right, divorce it. And don't forget the ceremony. Tell yourself something like, "I've decided to withdraw my commitment to this particular intention because, all things considered, it's no longer in my best interest to pursue it."

Granted, the "D" word is never pretty. But compared to the usual approach of letting estranged intentions fade away, divorcing intentions that just don't work out is a breath of fresh air.

Curing a Trigger Finger

I (Steve) can do about 90 percent of my home repairs. I don't mean that I can repair 90 percent of the things in my home that need fixing. What I mean is that I can complete about 90 percent of each job that I start! When it comes to installing a new faucet or rewiring a light switch, 90 percent is not good enough. Try to get water out of a faucet that's been 90 percent installed. Try to operate a light with a switch that's 90 percent wired. Ask my family. They've tried both.

I've left repair jobs unfinished because I discovered too late that I lacked all the knowledge, skills, and time required to complete the job. And I've put off starting many a home repair project because, after optimistically buying everything I needed to make the repair, I regained my senses and—appropriately—lost my confidence.

As monuments to this phenomenon, I own an unopened ten-gallon pail of "wall goop" I purchased about eight years ago to repair some cracks on the stairwell walls, and a "high-tech" outdoor security light, still in the original sealed carton, with a sale sticker on it that says $39.95. The list price today is $13.95!

The more I've learned about how the mind treats good intentions, the more I've come to appreciate why I and so many other people have a place in their homes—and a place in their lives—where monuments to poor follow through accumulate.

For years, my desire to save money and to enjoy a sense of self-reliance drove me to make promises I realistically couldn't keep. I'd see something that needed fixing or would be inspired by an interesting home improvement item on sale, and I'd immediately tune in only to the benefits of doing it myself. Only after punctuating a hasty promise with a hasty purchase would I tune in to the very good reasons why actually doing it myself was a really bad idea. And by that time, I'd already feel too committed to acknowledge that there really was no chance at all that I'd ever get the job done. So I'd just let the promise sit there forever on the bulging and burdensome "jobs pending" list.

I can honestly say that I am now much more careful than I used to be about making promises to myself, especially when it comes to home repairs. I still find myself *reflexively* tuning in to the benefits of doing it myself. But now, before I make any promises, I almost always *deliberately* tune in to the reasons why I shouldn't do it myself. And on the rare occasion that I do slip and make a foolish promise, I promptly admit my mistake, cut my losses, and take the commitment off the jobs pending list.

Life is sure a lot easier without a jobs pending list that's filled with items that you know in your heart you'll never complete.

CHAPTER 22

Making the Transition to a Follow Through Mindset

Perhaps the most valuable result of all education is the ability to make yourself do the thing you have to do when it ought to be done, whether you like it or not. It is the first lesson that ought to be learned; and however early a man's training begins, it is probably the last lesson that he learns thoroughly.

—Thomas Huxley

Part I: From Crutches to Tools

"These follow through strategies work great!" said Jan, a successful entrepreneur. "I'm keeping many more of the promises I make to myself and others, and I'm a lot better off because of it. Just ask my staff, or my husband, or my kids! It's been a blessing.

"That's why I'm embarrassed to admit that there's a part of me that wants to reject everything I've learned about following through! There's this little voice inside me that says, 'Grow up, Jan. Where's your pride? If you're really serious about doing something, then for crying out loud, you *should* just do it! You shouldn't need any of these silly gimmicks. They're just crutches. If you want it badly enough, you should have enough willpower to do it on your own.' "

Perhaps you recognize Jan's little "Should" voice. It's the official voice of the Follow Through Fairy Tale—that irresistibly appealing notion that good intentions magically produce good results; that "wanting it badly enough" is all it takes to get it done; and that the only remedy you need for failing is to "try harder next time."

To the Follow Through Fairy Tale, *crutch* is a dirty word.

By referring to these follow through strategies as crutches, Jan's little "Should" voice is accusing her of being both lazy and stupid. The voice is implying that, not only doesn't Jan really need "outside help," but that by relying on it, she's doing herself a great disservice. "These crutches will prevent you from exercising your own inner resources—your willpower and your self-discipline," the voice scolds. "How can you possibly expect to fully develop your own abilities if you rely on outside help?"

The little voice in Jan's head—and the Follow Through Fairy Tale it speaks for—is right about one thing and wrong about everything else. In one sense, follow through strategies *are* crutches.

But so what? At this stage in human evolution, we need all the help we can get.

Clinging to the belief that you can follow through by relying on inner resources alone is a lot like clinging to the belief that you can fly by flapping your arms. Both are appealing ideas—tempting fantasies. But mistake either for a doable option, and you'll fall flat on your face.

Not only do we *need* help from follow through strategies, the idea that relying on such help will harm us in some way is pure hogwash. Sure, it's true that if you rely unnecessarily on crutches to help you walk, you can deprive your muscles of exercise they need. But if you rely on a follow through strategy to help you follow through, the only thing you'll deprive yourself of is another follow through failure!

The truth is, there's not a shred of evidence to suggest that relying on outside help to follow through can in any way weaken your inner resources. On the contrary, what we've seen over and over again is that people who learn how to use follow through strategies effectively come to enjoy greater access to their own talents and abilities. They report having a keen and satisfying sense of being the captain of their own ship.

So, little "Should" voice, you can refer to follow through strategies as crutches if you want. But to people who have learned to use them well, follow through strategies are about as much like crutches as paintbrushes were crutches to Leonardo da Vinci. Leonardo was certainly "guilty" of relying on brushes to paint his masterpieces. But rather than holding back his inner resources, brushes were "tools" that enabled him to make magnificent use of his talent. And instead of gazing at the *Mona Lisa* and thinking, "Sure, it's a beautiful painting, but da Vinci cheated. He used brushes." We simply gaze and think, "What an amazing talent."

The right tools never hold your abilities back; they allow you to go further with the abilities you have. Whether it's an artist's brush or a follow through strategy, using tools to get better results is not cheating; it's not being lazy; and it's not being stupid. It's just being smart.

So the next time you're getting ready to use a follow through strategy and you hear that little "Should" voice inside ask, "Where's your pride?" proudly tell the voice, "My pride is in getting the job done."

Part II: From Inside-Out to Outside-In

You'd think the success Jan achieved by using follow through strategies would have been enough to silence the voice of the Follow Through Fairy Tale. But the Follow Through Fairy Tale isn't like all the other fairy tales we're encouraged to believe in as children and then encouraged to shed as we grow older. What's different about the Follow Through Fairy Tale is that we, as "grown-ups," are *still* being encouraged to believe in it!

We live in a culture that's in love with the idea of being inner-directed. We're bombarded with messages that teach us that "we have what it takes"—that "we can do anything if we try hard enough." We watch movie after movie where a hero or heroine, thanks only to a crystal clear vision, a burning desire, and an iron will, defies the odds to achieve an impossible goal. We find nothing more inspiring than stories of people who reach deep, deep inside and come up with whatever it takes to make their dreams come true. Such stories are as universally appealing as a beautiful sunset. They stir our emotions and invite us to follow suit—to look inward for solutions.

The problem is that our love affair with inner-directedness blinds us to the powerful role that outside influences can play in our lives. When we hear accounts of people doing "the impossible," we think, "Wow, the awesome power of talent and determination!" What we fail to notice, however, is the awesome power of outside influences to bring our inner resources fully to life.

Occasionally we get a fleeting glimpse of the vitally important but well-camouflaged role that outside influences play in our success. For example, in reflecting on his own success, basketball legend Magic Johnson once said of his chief competitor, "Larry Bird made Magic Johnson the best that Magic Johnson could be."

Unfortunately, such glimpses are few and far between. We don't have time for them. We're too busy teaching and learning the Follow Through Fairy Tale. And it's not just in the movies and in our sports arenas that it's "taught." It's taught everywhere. It's taught in popular magazines and in the overflowing self-improvement section of bookstores. It's taught in the most expensive and sophisticated seminars and workshops for sales people and executives. And it's taught both "live" and on tape by those merry messengers of the Follow Through Fairy Tale known as "motivational speakers."

Imagine, as an adult, attending workshop after workshop, reading book after book, listening to tape after tape, hearing speaker after speaker tell you that there really is a Santa Claus. It's just a harmless fairy tale, right? Well, there's a point where the fairy tale stops being harmless and starts being dangerous.

There's certainly no harm in believing in a jolly old man who knows everything and loves children. But when you start counting on Santa to actually bring gifts for your family, you've gone too far!

Likewise, the Follow Through Fairy Tale is harmless until you count on your inner resources *alone* to make sure that you'll follow through on your good intentions. Just as it's fine to believe in Santa as long as you make a point of buying the gifts yourself, it's fine to believe in the power of inner resources as long as you also make a point of using whatever outside help you need to get the job done.

So, by all means, go ahead and reach inside for all the inspiration, willpower, talent, vision, and determination you have. God knows, these are absolutely precious resources. But unless you're just making an inspirational movie, don't stop there! If you really want to make your dreams come true, reach *outside* too. Line up all the help you can get for the tough job of following through. It's better to get the job done with outside help than not to get it done at all.

Part III: From Double Standard to Single Standard

When it comes to following through on our good intentions, the message our culture sends is loud and clear: "Real achievement comes only from within." It couldn't be any clearer if the warning "No crutches allowed" flashed constantly in the sky for all to see.

We humans open up wide and swallow the "Up with inner resources" epigram whole. We buy hook, line, and sinker into what we call the Doctrine of Inside-Out. It's the belief that success is a pure, unadulterated expression of inner resources.

But without realizing it, we're guilty of adopting a double standard. While we seem to embrace *Inside-Out* when it comes to ourselves, we don't buy it at all when we want someone else to succeed.

The fact of the matter is, we preach Inside-Out, but when it comes to helping others succeed, we practice *Outside-In*. In other words, we never hesitate to recognize and rely on outside influences to bring out the very best in *other* people.

Just ask any teacher, or coach, or boss, or parent.

Teachers may value their students' inner resources. But you won't find many teachers who count on Inside-Out to get their students to learn and succeed. Homework, exams, term papers, grades, detention, "gold stars," and the time-honored threat of a trip to the principal's office are just a few of the Outside-In tools that teachers use every day to help their students behave in certain ways.

Coaches give great speeches about "inner drive." But find a coach who counts only on athletes' inner drive to win a championship, and we'll show you a coach who's unemployed. Coaches rely on Outside-In tools all the time. Inner drive is great. But inner drive with mandatory practices, team rules, pep talks, and lots of one-on-one coaching is what brings out the best in athletes.

Sales managers urge members of their sales force to reach deep inside. "Be a self-starter," they plead. "Grab the ball and run with it." They sure talk a good Inside-Out game. But most managers know better than to count on Inside-Out. They put most of their eggs in the Outside-In basket. They rely on quotas, bonuses, contests—all Outside-In tools—to keep their people moving.

And then, of course, there are parents. No matter how much parents believe in and cherish their child's inner resources, they wouldn't dream of relying on Inside-Out alone. Parents use Outside-In constantly. They carefully choose and aggressively arrange outside influences in an effort to bring out the very best in their child. They try to choose the right schools, the right teachers, the right friends, the right neighborhoods, the right movies, the right *everything*. Heck, using Outside-In is what parenting is all about!

So when it comes to influencing *other* people's behavior, we definitely get it. We know that Inside-Out is not enough. We understand the power of Outside-In. And we're not afraid to use it.

To follow through consistently, you don't have to disregard your inner resources. You just have to discard the Double Standard. You have to realize that it's not just what's on the inside that determines whether you'll follow through. It's what's on the outside too. You have to recognize the power of Outside-In and be willing to use it—freely, boldly, creatively—to influence *your* own behavior.

It's an interesting paradox: The key to being successfully inner-directed is to take full advantage of how outer-directed you are.

Part IV: From Knee-Jerk Freedom to Real Freedom

There may be another little voice in your head that urges you to reject what you've learned about following through. It's hard to talk back to this voice because it's hard to think of it as being anything but on your side. The voice we're referring to is the "voice of freedom."

The voice of freedom speaks from deep, deep inside. It speaks from way below the level of conscious thinking. It speaks from the level of reflexes.

To the voice of freedom, life is simple. "Freedom is good. Restrictions are bad." That's all there is to it.

The voice of freedom is utterly obsessed with keeping your options wide open. It hates when you close any doors. It bristles when you let yourself get pinned down. It rolls its eyes when you accept anything "with strings attached." It gets prickly whenever you go down a one-way street. And it goes absolutely ballistic when you *deliberately* restrict yourself.

The voice of freedom is passionate but primitive. It can't grasp the idea that accepting a restriction *now* may be the best way—and sometimes the only way—to achieve greater freedom *later*. "A restriction is a restriction," the voice insists.

The voice of freedom regards follow through strategies as a threat. "Stay away from them," the voice insists. "Can't you see, those strategies restrict your freedom!" the voice shouts.

Well, in one sense, the voice is right to be threatened. Follow through strategies *will* restrict your freedom. They'll restrict your freedom to fail!

Freedom is often the enemy of follow through, not its ally. Too much freedom prevents you from getting the job done.

Suppose, for example, you want to free yourself from the bondage of being overweight. The voice of freedom hears "Free," and it's behind you all the way—all the way, that is, until you accept any of the restrictions that you have to accept in order to lose weight. For example, consider keeping foods you shouldn't eat out of your home, and the voice of freedom will object. "You can't do that," the voice insists. "That's restricting your freedom!" Consider promising your grandmother that as a gift for her ninetieth birthday, you'll get rid of those fifteen pounds she knows the doctor urged you to lose. The voice of freedom will object again. "You can't do that!" the voice shouts. "Don't commit yourself. Don't make a promise. Don't get yourself pinned down. Leave your options open."

The voice of freedom is too shortsighted to be anything but an obstacle to following through. So listen carefully for it. And when you hear it urging you to reject what you've learned about following through, talk back.

Tell the voice that the road to real freedom is paved with the right restrictions.

Epilogue

*When you get right down to the root meaning of the word
succeed, you find that it simply means to follow through.*

—F. W. Nichol

We wrote this book because we feel passionately about helping people follow through. We admit that we set the bar high: *To change forever the way people experience and treat their own good intentions.*

Only you can judge how well we did.

If you still believe that *having* a good intention is all it takes to implement it, we've failed miserably. If, on the other hand, you now understand that to follow through consistently you have to recognize, accept, correct, and keep on correcting for the mind's design problems, we've done okay. And, of course, if you put down this book and start using our strategies to follow through like never before, we can congratulate ourselves on a job well done.

But we won't be fully satisfied with what we've accomplished unless, along with learning *how* to follow through, you've developed a deeper appreciation of *why* to follow through. If we haven't convinced you that investing in your ability to follow through is one of the wisest investments you can make in your own future, we've failed you.

You see, following through is not just about getting things done. It's about being the captain of your own ship. It's about more than what you *do* in life. It's about how you *feel* about your life.

Carrie's husband, Rich, knows exactly what we mean:

Carrie and I have been married for fourteen years. This is the first time that she's ever cried at the breakfast table. She feels trapped in an unsatisfying job that's going nowhere. She feels so miserable and hopeless. I feel awful for her.

As we sat down to eat breakfast yesterday, I could tell right away that something was wrong. As Carrie started to speak, her voice was trembling, she looked scared, and before long, tears were rolling down her cheeks. "Rich," she said to me, "it hit me like a ton of bricks this morning. My career is a mess. I let the window of opportunity close one time too many. And I'm afraid it'll never open for me again.

"What hurts the most," Carrie continued, "is that I know I have no one but myself to blame for the depressing mess I'm in. I've had so many opportunities to make things better. I can't believe that I let every one of them slip away."

As much as I tried to comfort her, I couldn't really disagree with the facts. Poor follow through has always been Carrie's downfall. It's what's always kept her from making her dreams come true.

I love Carrie. I want her to be happy. I'd do anything

to help. But I feel so helpless. I get sick when I think about what will happen to her—and us—if she keeps dropping the ball. I'm worried that she'll have a mess of regrets to carry with her for the rest of her life.

That's right, Rich. Following through is not just about getting things done. It's about preventing regrets. It's about being ready and able to take advantage of opportunity when it knocks. It's about making the best possible use of your own abilities and talents to build a satisfying life.

Following through in real life has nothing to do with fairy tales. But it has everything to do with making your dreams come true.

About the Authors

Steve Levinson, Ph.D. is a clinical psychologist, inventor, and entrepreneur. Born and raised in New York City, he earned a bachelors degree in psychology from Queens College and a doctorate in clinical psychology from the University of Rochester before moving to Minnesota to direct an innovative rural mental health program that has flourished under his leadership for the past twenty five years.

Dr. Levinson has been studying the problem of poor follow through for most of his career. He is the inventor of the Motiv-Aider®, an electronic device he created to help people follow through consistently on their own good intentions. He is also president of Behavioral Dynamics, Inc., a company he co-founded in 1987 to develop, manufacture and market the MotivAider® worldwide to businesses, schools, health care institutions, and individuals.

Dr. Levinson is a popular speaker and consultant who combines his talents as a psychologist and innovator with a passion for helping organizations and individuals follow through.

Pete Greider, M.Ed. is a consultant who helps athletes and business people overcome obstacles to peak performance. He earned a bachelor's degree in communication from Michigan State University and his Masters in Education from the University of New Hampshire.

Mr. Greider has been a sports psychology consultant for such professional teams as the Orlando Magic and a business consultant for various national corporations, including Northwestern Mutual Life, General Electric, and State Farm Insurance.

Having concluded that the biggest obstacle to peak performance is poor follow through, Mr. Greider focuses on helping his individual and business clients adopt effective strategies for following through. He is a popular keynote speaker whose credits include Exxon, Northwestern Mutual Life, the Million Dollar Round Table, and the U.S. Chamber of Commerce.

Contact Information:

Steve Levinson, Ph.D.
Behavioral Dynamics, Inc.
P.O. Box 66
Thief River Falls, MN 56701

Pete Greider, M.Ed.
Pete Greider & Associates
556 Shawnee Trail
Blacksburg, VA 24060

You can contact both authors via email at followingthrough@yahoo.com.